ALPHA LADDERS

CAPTAIN OF YOUR DESTINY

by LINKEDIN AND TOWN HALL ACHIEVER OF THE YEAR
EY NOMINEE ENTREPRENEUR OF THE YEAR
GRAND HOMAGE LYS DIVERSITY

Dr. BAK NGUYEN, DMD

&

JONAS DIOP

TO EVERYONE LOOKING TO MASTER THEIR MIND AND SKILL
TO GAIN INFLUENCE AND POWER. THOSE ARE THE WORDS
IN POPULAR CULTURE. IN TRUTH, THE RIGHT WORDING IS
TO FIND USEFULNESS.

by Dr. BAK NGUYEN

ISBN: 978-1-989536-56-8

ABOUT THE AUTHORS

From Canada, **Dr BAK NGUYEN**, Nominee Ernst and Young Entrepreneur of the year, Grand Homage Lys DIVERSITY, and LinkedIn & TownHall Achiever of the year. Dr Bak is a cosmetic dentist, CEO and founder of Mdex & Co. His company is revolutionizing the dental field. Speaker and motivator, he wrote 72 books over 36 months accumulating many world records (to be officialized).

- **ENTREPRENEURSHIP**
- **LEADERSHIP**
- **QUEST OF IDENTITY**
- **DENTISTRY AND MEDICINE**
- **PARENTING**
- **CHILDREN BOOKS**
- **PHILOSOPHY**

In 2003, he founded Mdex, a dental company upon which in 2018, he launched the most ambitious private endeavour to reform the dental industry, Canada wide. Philosopher, he has close to his heart the quest of happiness of the people surrounding him, patients and colleagues alike. In 2020, he launched an International collaborative initiative named **THE ALPHAS** to share knowledge and for Entrepreneurs and Doctors to thrive through the Greatest Pandemic and Economic depression of our time.

In 2016, he co-found with Tranie Vo, Emotive World Incorporated, a tech research company to use technology to empower happiness and sharing. U.A.X. the ultimate audio experience is the landmark project on which the team is advancing, utilizing the technics of the movie industry and the advancement in ARTIFICIAL INTELLIGENCE to save the book industry and to upgrade the continuing education space.

These projects have allowed Dr Nguyen to attract interests from the international and diplomatic community and he is now the center of a global discussion in the wellbeing and the future of the health profession. It is in that matter that he shares his thoughts and encourages the health community to share their own stories.

"It's not worth it go through it alone! Together, we stand, alone, we fall."

Motivational speaker and serial entrepreneur, philosopher and author, from his own words, Dr Nguyen describes himself as a dentist by circumstances, an entrepreneur by nature and a communicator by passion.

He also holds recognitions from the Canadian Parliament and the Canadian Senate.

From France, **JONAS DIOP**, Author-speaker, business strategist and leadership expert. Jonas Diop has already impacted the lives of entrepreneurs, high-level athletes as well as individuals thanks to his ability to awaken the best that lies dormant in everyone.

His mantra is always one step closer.

The so-called Empire Builder is known for his great energy and outspokenness, he is committed to ensuring that everyone can reach their full potential. Invested for over 15 years in personal growth, he has synthesized the essence of the best in their field in order to bring them to you.

Certified professional coach, NLP technician (Neuro-Linguistic Programming) He is also a member of the Club des entrepreneurs francophones du Canada.

Since 2017, he launched the podcast #DUC: Deviens Un Conquérant. From his atypical history, he knows the secret in order to achieve success.

www.JonasDiop.com

ALPHA LADDERS

CAPTAIN OF YOUR DESTINY

by Dr. BAK NGUYEN
& JONAS DIOP

INTRODUCTION
BY Dr BAK NGUYEN

CONCLUSION
BY Dr BAK NGUYEN

INTRODUCTION
by Dr. BAK NGUYEN

The last time that I wrote an introduction was a few weeks ago. By then, I just finished writing and publishing my 73rd book, **TOUCHSTONE, LEVERAGING TODAY'S PSYCHOLOGICAL SMOG**, co-written with Dr. Ken Serota.

In the last introduction, I was hoping for Barnes and Noble to pick it up and distribute it. Well, it is done! A few days after Amazon accepted the book, Barnes and Noble made it available in their library. That's my 13th book distributed by Barnes and Noble. Can I hope for a permanent bridge? The next book will tell.

The last introduction was **COVIDCONOMICS**, about 2 weeks ago. Usually, you should expect me to announce that the writing was intense and intoxicating and that it would be available soon… but no.

COVIDCONOMICS is a long term book. With the world phenomenon that we need to empower, **COVIDCONOMICS** will take at least a few months to be completed. I gave myself the dateline of the beginning of August 2021, just in time to be part of my next world record of writing 100 books within 4 years.

Yes, that is the next step. And I am so far behind. So far, this year, **TOUCHSTONE** was my first to come out. And it was the only one in the first quarter of my fourth year. If **COVIDCONOMICS** will be taking months to write, how do I reconcile both my challenges, writing the next world record and changing the world for the better?

It was clear that whatever I was doing is now merely sufficient, even my momentum and tornado power will need tweaking to achieve this one. I will have to write multiple books simultaneously.

Writing books, I now can say that I know how. I learned on the field. But creating a movement of unity and inspire change, that is something we talk about for years… and that I haven't achieved yet.

Do I inspire people? I surely hope so, I know that I am not leaving people indifferent. The signs are now too obvious to miss, even by me. Do they stand up and walk their own destiny from the motivation and inspiration I gave them? That's another question, one much less easy to answer.

The story, too often repeats itself. As people discover me, they are mesmerized and charmed. Then, they want to connect. As they get closer, I treat them as colleagues and peers. I lead by example, so as I empower them, I will also be the first one to walk the new path. This is where most stay behind.

Those closest to me, well, I lend them a hand and they are walking right behind me, on the path that I just created. I like to say that they are walking beside me, but reality is hard to change. As soon as I stop walking, they stop too, turn around, or are simply lost.

"Great leaders create other leaders, not followers."

I am not sure who said that, but it got me at my core, years ago. Now facing my own journey, I must admit that I might be a leader, leading by example, but I am no great leader since I failed to produce leaders. I attract great leaders and mentors; the creation of the **ALPHAS** and of my **BOARD OF DIRECTORS** are proofs of my magnetism.

I shared and entertain people with true stories and my take on Life, but so far, I have **FANS** that I do not know and **JEALOUSY** that keeps polluting my vibe and ripple effect. That's my impact.

When you take the time to think about it, it is not that hard to understand. People are attracted to my bold move and impact. They are inspired. Then, they want to join. I welcome them. And here is where it gets messy. As I welcome them as peers and equals, it is now up to them to walk their talk.

"The kind of talk that I empower are bold, vast, and free.
Walking these words takes more than inspiration.
It takes commitment."
Dr. Bak Nguyen

And very quickly, what was a genuine desire to connect morphed into the need to compare and to bring me down. It is ironic to say that we are all the instrument of the jealousy we suffer.

I suffered that pain for decades, as I was trying to help everyone, and waiting for everyone to come on board. Now, I know all too well, that not everyone will come on board and will embrace the adventure, even if they sign up for and paid all the entry tickets.

So I embraced a new philosophy, to open the door and to lead, going faster and faster. Moving faster was the way for me to leave before jealousy could set down and corrupt my vibe. Jealousy can only be effective as you can see and touch the other party. Well, at my speed, good luck to keep me in sight...

That was the perfect recipe since it was either that I remain a great model to that person, and they are following me from a distance, so no jealousy; or if the jealousy is maintained, that person is running not too far from me, matching my pace. The only problem is that it isn't friendly.

"I am in it for the fun. I get my fun sharing and scoring."
Dr. Bak Nguyen

Even those with whom I enjoy the company and who enjoy mine, well, it is nearly impossible for them to keep the pace for

a long moment. And then, the inevitable occurs: I accelerate…
leaving them too, behind.

It will be a lonely ride to follow such a recipe. Fortunately
enough, I have my companions: Generals, and Lieutenants,
and the fans I do not know about. The mentors and Alphas are
attracted by what I am and do. With them, I have a great time
sharing.

My lieutenants are my proteges and sometimes employees. I
have their respect and they produce their part of work to
materialize my views and ideas. But if I spend too much time
close with any of them, I run the risk of burning them with my
vision and vibe…

So I learned to keep a safe distance. Even my proteges have to
space out their encounters with me to keep the harmony for
both their sake and mine. Standing too close to me daily can
be very intimidating.

That hurts me to my core since I have no alternate desire than
to see a great leader emerge from that soul I touch and care
about. Since I will not stop writing more and more books, that
is now my new reality. What about the next phase of evolution?

I lead by example and set world records doing so. Now that I
am looking for more, and for better, I am looking to see those I
touch to set their own record, world record, or personal
record, I am looking to see great leaders emerging, not just
followers, fans, and haters.

COVIDCONOMICS will be the best platform to apply such philosophy. I will attract the elite and Alphas of the world and we will map the future. And the people? This is where I am facing a cliff… to bridge.

Joining me are two of my trusted lieutenants, strategist Jonas Diop and International Counsellor, Brenda Garcia. Both my proteges, Jonas and Brenda, have come to understand my essence and are empowering it with all of their skills, talents, and hopes.

They understand me, but much more, they understand the others, those in my ripple effect, those fans I touched. Quickly fans will grow into either followers or haters. I am looking for neither, I am looking for genuine friendships.

It is now clear that left untouched, my impact and ripple effect will not be the one I am hoping for. So with the love, friendship, and trust shared with my lieutenants, I will force myself to build what I despite: structure and hierarchy.

That is the only way to build and to empower more and more people to find their way to their own destiny. But I will not be doing that lightly. I will push the conversation to its source, if there is a structure, it has to be justified and relevant in nowaday's context.

My consolation is that I will be spending time with Jonas and Brenda, friends that I love and enjoy the company. My hope is that they will be emerging from loyal lieutenants to captains, stirring their own ships, projects, and destiny.

And with their help, you might too. **ALPHAS LADDERS** is my bridge to you, all of you. My job is to keep scoring and open new ways and possibilities, walking my legend.

The bridges and **ALPHAS LADDERS** will organize my essence, life force and experiences so you can all walk my step as template to embrace your own **DESTINY**.

This is **ALPHA LADDERS**, Captain of your destiny.

DESTINY is not something we received,
But something we write and rewrite
Dr. BAK NGUYEN

CHAPTER 1

AMONGST ALPHAS

by JONAS DIOP

For once, let's start with the end: you have a fabulous treasure in your hands. For you to be enriched with wisdom, I have to use my special interrogation skill over and over again.

Indeed, I have become an expert in the art of extracting the essence of great minds by deciphering the dialogue, the tone of voice, the posture, going as far as theirs silences.

My mission is simple, to provide you with the tools and testimonials of those who did it, who met the challenges of the impossible, and map the way so you can do it too. You too can create your **world of possibilities**.

I have known Dr. Bak for almost 3 years. What I really appreciate about him is his pragmatism and his outspokenness. You have to combine the useful with the pleasant, to keep overachieving. You do it because it is fun. As the saying goes:

"Lift up with ambition, lay down with satisfaction."

As visionaries, our belief systems align. Some thought we were crazy, until we showed it was just extravaganza. Dr. Bak, to purge himself of his emotions, started writing for 36 months. He is now over 74 books. This is his 75th.

We are not looking for honors but to leave a mark. I went from an immigrant to a leading business strategist advising top personalities and athletes. Dr. Bak went from dentist to CEO to world record author. Can these success stories be duplicated, over and over again? This is the big question that we will be tackling in this journey, the **ALPHA LADDERS**.

***

It's Wednesday, December 9, 2020. I wake up. It's freezing cold outside with the arrival of the first snow. I told myself: "Today will be a great day as we are going to lay the foundations for Project **STELLAR**."

I visualize all the details of **STELLAR**. It has been with me for over a decade. To finally be able to put it into orbit is what's pushing me out of my bed with hope and enthusiasm. I know that **STELLAR** is pure gold. It is the secrets, and steps to build a business megastructure from A to Z, turnkey.

Just imagine being in Elon Musk's head with his Space X project, having this vision that we could colonize Mars. I take my Rooibos with honey and lemon in front of a YouTube video that narrates his journey from a dreamer to the light of being the second richest man in the world, dethroning Bill Gates.

I too, dream of contributing my stone to Humanity, leaving a better world behind, and helping people to be happier. I get ready. I put on my scarf and my mask, and make my way to the Mdex headquarters, downtown Montreal. It is 9:37 AM.

At 10:03 AM, I am there, on the 5th floor of the Scotia Tower. I walk into the Mdex offices, looking for the main astronaut, the commander of the mission. I find him at his writing desk, he is focused. I do not want to disrupt his concentration.

Suddenly he stops. Not even taking his eyes away from his computer screen, he announces yet another victory, another milestone on his way to freeing people from fear. And our conversation starts.

He is named amongst the 100 most brilliant doctors in the world. He had become a dentist for the love of his parents. He remained a loved dentist for his patients. Changing the world from a dental chair, that was the title of his first published book, now, it is a reality that he keeps forging and growing with each passing day.

Looking at my mentor, brother, and friend, I was scratching my head to know how can the **STELLAR** protocol enhance his speed, reach, and impact? To do it better, faster? To reach more people to free themselves from **FEAR**, procrastination, doubts, and excuses? I see so much power and kindness in this man, I have to extract his essence to help everyone willing to challenge themselves to become their best version. This is my mission!

Fifteen minutes into our intense conversation, he left the room to attend to his next patient. I settled into one of the offices, working on my Trello board, on the blueprint of the ALPHAS, Dr. Bak's community.

I was expecting Brenda, she was supposed to arrive around noon. Together we will refine Bak's message. It's 12:09, we start our three-way meeting with Brenda, Dr. Bak, and myself. Question after question, the wording had to be untied in order to fill in the boxes of the **STELLAR** table, to define the shape of Dr. Bak in the eye of the public.

By now, we know his strengths, speed, and impact. Dr. Bak's natural attribute is the wind. He has no power animal, the wind and being shapeless are his essence. One capable of being peaceful like a light breeze on your face, but also one that can become a tornado capable of uprooting trees. Dr. Bak can surprise you and bring you to new heights when you least expected it.

What we appreciate amongst us, is the dialectic or even as we call it, the art of the argument. We sometimes have different points of view. And here comes the interesting exchanges, as we argue and point out the different alternatives to a problem. That, we call **perspectives**.

We have a deep respect for one another, but we also hold our stances firmly, as we have a strong value system. Luckily in between the two of us stood Brenda, a brilliant mind ensuring diplomacy and cohesion.

Brenda greatly facilitates the communication. She grasped the subtleties that might have escaped us in the heat of the exchange, rephrase them with a light questioning, adding her touch and comments.

She has been Dr. Bak's right hand for the last 4 years, in between her master's degree in international diplomacy. She knows the man and how he works, but moreover, she understands his thoughts as she has worked on most of his books.

We were in turmoil when Steve came by to say hi. It was, indeed, lunch time for over 30 minutes. He arrived with a delicious Quinoa salad. Steve is an expert in social media and brand positioning. He is quite a creative mind. Steve is also the producer behind the Alpha classes that Dr. Bak and myself are launching.

The four of us met to think and to draft the message and image of Dr. Bak as a brand. Ideas were flying in all directions. We were operating like a band, pushing one another to go beyond their limits. It works because we have a deep bond of friendship and common benevolence binding us.

Each idea has the potential to be amplified and to become a new project if we allow it to express itself and to journey to its maturity in our minds.

This intensive brainstorming called for a break to restore. Today no Bagel for me, because I am on a diet. The others would take advantage of it on my behalf. I needed strength for the battle, vitamins and omega 3s, I had in my lunch box, a slice of lasagna made the day before, an avocado, a banana, and a bottle of water. My portions were smaller now to avoid the early afternoon slump from digestion.

It was 1:28 PM when I finished my lunch. I had a 30-minute strategic consulting session. Finally, around 2:00 PM, we were on fire understanding how Dr. Bak can share his journey and help as many people as possible to free themselves from the chains of their fears and take control of their lives.

Everyone has idealistic ideas and the potential to remake the world differently, hopefully, better. I saw Dr. Bak do it again and again. What I can tell you is that nothing is impossible nor out of reach. We only need to change some of our behaviors, to leave some of our preconceived beliefs.

Different assumptions, clash of ideologies. Nothing is good, nothing is wrong. I truly believe that our duty is to give them a structure, so that people can evolve step by step once they are inspired. That's me.

For Dr. Bak, the message is the key importance. Everyone has needs and desires, it is for each of us to make peace with what we want, what we need, and what's available. Dr. Bak has the power to reach abundance, from a single vision. He is sharing his journey and how he creates such abundance, but that isn't simple to reproduce to most of us.

Some of us, not to say, most of us, are still wandering. Is it okay to trigger someone? Is it okay to allow ourselves to interfere in someone's life, for the good of that person?

Dr. Bak is strongly against interfering. In his words, he is a doctor, and he can only treat the people giving him consent. But what about those too fearful to do so? The needs are overwhelming, and yet, they will need help to open up.

That's my view. I want theirs best, so I need to give them the tools. But is that condescension or empathy? This is the kind of conversation we have as mentor and protege, as friends, as brothers.

I keep telling myself that I am giving a message they'll understand and look forward to. But is that hypocrisy, respect, or compassion? On the one hand, ethics and deontology, on the other, human beings and feelings.

If we want to empower them to grow and be different, we need to give them structure. Bak hates structures. He spent the last decades of his life, fleeing from the structures holding him down.

We were debating. Steve had to leave. Brenda balanced and got the best out of us. We were having an intense argument but I wanted to get the verses out of Bak's nose about his methodology, the ladders and daily to achieve his success and to keep overachieving.

Suddenly this question appeared in my head: how did you manage to click? What triggered THE change? He confessed that everything started when one of his mentors told him to forgive himself.

It was this phrase that got to him, to his core. First, that caused a reaction of rejection, then, one of disgust, and finally, one of anger. Why was this innocuous sentence so powerful on his emotions?

Luckily, Dr. Bak is very self-aware. He decided to dig into the question, to understand what there was to forgive, and why his violent reaction to the proposal. The story of that journey is for him to share with you. What I can tell you is that he managed to forgive himself and others in order to reconcile with his inner being.

He finally understood my point of view. From that, emerged the book that you are now holding in your hands. I want to know, feel, and understand Dr. Bak's awakening and each of the stages that he had to pass by to become the Dr. Bak we now know and love.

More than that, I want to map the journey, the emotions, and the mindset so each of us can now walk through the same path, as we each have to meet our destiny.

It took years to get to this point. Here are the four questions I will have answers to:

1. How did he find his reconstruction point?
2. How did he manage to find the resources to have a leverage effect on his life?
3. What type of emotional intelligence one needs to receive, listen to, and above all, how to implement the advice received?
4. What is still fuelling his drive, ambition, and how to maintain it?

I will have my friend and mentor, Dr. Bak to answer without filter, in the light of his elements, his experience, his feelings.

Ladies and gentlemen, welcome to the ALPHAS, I hope this book will help you on your journey. It can be a shining reminder. Just know that we are your supporters.

This is **ALPHA LADDERS**, Captain of your destiny.

DESTINY is not something we received,
But something we write and rewrite
Dr. BAK NGUYEN

CHAPTER 2
THE TRIGGER

by Dr. BAK NGUYEN

Let's start with the Elephant in the room, shall we? Jonas dropped a bomb when he mentioned that question in his chapter a little earlier on, how did I click? What woke me up from a dentist to a tornado.

Half a decade ago, my country was facing a political crisis. Social equilibria were about to be broken facing 2 elections. The first one in particular got me at the core of my beliefs. I couldn't stand still watching the news and swallowing the policies made in my name, as a citizen. And this was way before COVID!

I stood up and put my fist on the table. Enough is enough. But then, I realized that I was to blame. Our leaders were those because people like me refuse to run. On the issue, by that time, I turned down twice within the last 18 years the possibility to run for office. At my first opening, I was barely 18. Then, I was 36.

I always thought that there were better people to run the country. And there were, for the last 18 years… But now, my country needed me. So I stood up and call my friends and the people I knew that could help me pave the way.

Amongst the phone calls I made that evening, Dr. Mohamed Benkhalifa, doctor in political science and lawyer was the person who took my cry for help very seriously. Dr. Benkhalifa is also a liaison between the NGO (non-governmental organizations) at the United Nations.

Prior to that call, Mohamed was a big brother to me. He is a man who understands power, its ladders, and organization. From that call, he became my mentor and coach.

I spent the next 9 months under his training. I learned much about organization, systems, justice, and above all, influence. At the height of our coaching, he was re-writing my education.

I must say that it was brutal. Not pleasant, not friendly, but necessary. I love this man with all of my heart, it wasn't the man who was brutal, it was the process. As much as I suffered from being a sensitive soul, trimmed and put in a box with bars to grow into a respected member of society, a doctor. The process of getting out of that box was even more painful.

It was that painful because everything happened so intensively within a very short time frame. From a man always laughing and always positive, I became a man that was swearing, especially in the presence of my coach. This is so not me, but I couldn't hold it back. It was that painful and disorientating.

One evening, he called me. He asked me to meet him at the top of the city, the Mount-Royal, a Mountain in the middle of Montreal. It was the middle of the summer. I took my brand new red convertible, a birthday gift from my wife, and met with my coach on the mountain.

I wasn't in a mood to be forged in the fire again. That's my body talking. My mind was pretty aware that I was the one asking for that training. I was the one paying! So I kept my opinion and complaints to myself and listen. To my surprise, it was very light as a conversation.

And then, out of the blue, Mohamed looked at me as I was focussing on the horizon and the lights of the city. He said:

"You have to forgive."
Dr. Mohamed Benkhalifa

Forgive what?! I replied. I have nothing to forgive. He smiled and added that I also need to forgive myself. This is where it became very interesting. Forgive my wording, but my exact words were: "What the fuck do I have to forgive myself for?!"

I was pissed and aggressive. It surprised me to my core. Even out of myself, I am a very respectful person, and Mohamed is amongst the people I hold in high esteem. It was simply not me talking.

I apologized and we called it a night. Mohamed seemed happy. He became very kind and told me to sleep on the subject. Driving home, I couldn't reconcile who I was with how I reacted. I slept on the intrigue.

A few hours later, it faded away. I could finally rest my eyes and my soul. What I thought was water under the bridge resurfaced a few days later, out of the blue, as I was attending to a patient. From the corner of my eye, I saw myself in the mirror, dressed with in doctor's white coat caring for my patient. That was very troubling.

From the day I became a good doctor, I learned to empty myself of my pride, identity, and problems, to be available to my patients and to solve their problems. That was my secret recipe.

As the **FORGIVENESS** resurfaced in my mind, the frustration and anger were following very, very closely. I maintain my posture, bit my tongue to hold the emotions in, and finished the operation.

It wasn't a hard procedure, but for the first time in years, I had a hard time delivering. It wasn't effortless and above the rules of time anymore. I felt each second of that operation on my soul, just like the clock ticking was poking my skin with its spear.

I sweated. When finally, I completed the operation, I went out to wash my face with cold water. Looking up, I saw the face of a stranger in the mirror. Everything around was fading out. Facing me was the look of a stranger waiting. The tension was building up.

It was like in those horror movies where the demons took over your soul. Well, it wasn't scary, it was ugly, it was disturbing. I was facing a stranger, and yet, I felt that familiarity. Then, a man was washing his hand next to me, that pulled me out of my trance.

Now that feeling of a stranger looking at me with familiar eyes was the only thing on my mind. Needless to say that the rest of the day was not an easy one, as I had my schedule full of surgical interventions.

That night, I slept very lightly. Every time that I closed my eye, I could see those familiar eyes looking back at me. I woke up many times to go wash my face with cold water.

I could not clearly remember if I was asleep or awake looking in the mirror, but it came to me. I saw the tunnel, a dark, humid and cold alley, with the wall narrowing down on you as you are stepping forward.

The air was heavy with humidity and that smell of rotting flesh. It wasn't pleasant, it was spooky, but not scary. I remember looking at my feet, I was bare feet, walking on black sand. I finally arrived in front of a cage.

To paint a clear image, if Lucifer was held in a cage in hell, this was a replica. The door was open and the cage was unoccupied. I stepped in. On the floor, a thick Persian rug was welcoming my feet. I felt the movements under my feet, but it was too dark to see clearly what was moving...

At the center of the room (yes, the cage was that big), was an old chest, made of wood and iron, covered with fur. I got closer and closer. As I got closer, the air was heavier and heavier. Never, it crossed my mind to look back, to look above my shoulder, I felt disgusted and would have given anything to be somewhere else, anywhere. But very very strangely, I felt safe.

I finally arrived within arm's reach of the chest. It wasn't locked. I opened it. I could not see since the shadow was thickening. The only thing that was sure was the odor. That smell of rotting flesh, well, it came from there. As I open the chest, it seems like decades of smell all came out, all at once. You know that feeling of crying was you are cutting onions? Well, the tears were the same from that smell.

It took me a while to recuperate. I cleared my eyes. I finally resolved myself to look into the chest. There were body parts. And the body parts were still moving, covered in blood and rotted flesh. I vomited.

That was very troubling. For the few next days, that was all I could think of. By night, I will come back again to the tunnel, and the cage, and the chest. From one trip to the next, the air lightens up and the shadow became thinner and thinner. It was still dark, humid, and disgusting, but it was known.

I finally had the chance to see clearly what was in the chest. It was my wings, those I have accepted the amputation, years ago. For that, I needed to forgive those who amputated me. But I gave my consent, I was part of the executioners. Then, the worst part is that I was the one who put the wings in the chest and sealed them from the world.

I closed my eye with pain. The tears, this time, were real, not from the smell nor the onions, but from the depth of my soul. I brought the chest back home with me.

Under the sun, the wings were healing slowly and the smell faded away gradually. Those parts are me. Looking back in the mirror, I saw that stranger looking back, but now, more at ease, at peace.

Contrary to the horror movie, there was no anger or frustration building up to a revenge scenario, just healing, and reunification. I healed and reunited with my inner-self, my sensitive soul, and creativity. Those were the wings I amputated.

A few weeks later, I met with my coach and mentor. I told him that I finally understood my reaction and what I needed to forgive myself for. He smiled, he was expecting that much from me.

As I was thanking him, he started with the next phase, of how we should forge my mind to become a leader of men... putting aside that sensitivity.

I did not feel anger or violence, I just felt that half of me, the re-united half was voicing up for the first time. That was a big NO. No way that my newly sketched and grafted wings were being clipped down once more. Mohamed never really understood what just happened, but that day started the end of our coaching relationship.

I still love the man dearly. Without his love and attention, never will I have reunited. But now that I was reunited, I was a different man, I was whole. Politic and to run for office lost all, all of its appeal, all at once. Playing the piano was now much more appealing and natural to me.

I thanked Mohamed and declined to run for the third time, even with all the resources and time dedicated to the cause. I broke his heart. Years later, he wrote to me at each election, wishing that I would have changed my mind. Each time, the refusal was more firm.

It took years to heal and to learn to walk again, whole. I made place for my creativity and my sensitivity, right beside my logic and boldness. My parents and society forged out of me a doctor, ethical, smart, and strong. Nature gave me sensitivity and creativity. Now it was for me to bridge them as my new whole.

I never held anyone responsible for my amputations, but myself. A few years later, as I discover my writing skills, I opened up more and more about Conformity and what it did to me. My parents, my teachers, society. Strangely enough, just like walking the tunnel bare feet, I do not feel any resentment. It wasn't pleasant, but it was familiar.

I talked and shared openly, and allowed time and sunlight to heal the wounds. As for myself, you saw me playing the piano and writing about it from time to time. Well, that's me, the sensitive part of me voicing up. I can tell you that my inner voice is becoming stronger and stronger. Today, I can play almost any song without practice, just listening, and following the musical flow.

Just give me the chords and let's play. Well, that was true in pop and RnB. I finally decoded Jazz, soft jazz, but as I got into blues… that is where I reached my limits. Yes, I have fun playing the piano, but it holds a deeper meaning.

Playing music has become the new gauge of my intelligence. Today, I am known for many things, but in the medical field, what I brought new to the table is **EMOTIONAL INTELLIGENCE**. Well, playing the piano is how I gauge my **EMOTIONAL INTELLIGENCE**.

Forgiving myself started the healing and reunification process, the journey ahead was still a long one until I learned to fly and used these amputated wings of mine.

What I want to shed the light on here are the trauma and pain. In the years following my reunification, I have undone, one by one, most of the forced values and training that decades of tears and sweat have forged. Even from the sacred fire of religion and family values, all the knobs melt and the flow of Life healed, even the unattached and amputated parts.

This chapter is very visceral, very personal. This is also why I am firmly against forcing liberation on anyone. You have to be the one walking your tunnel and welcoming what you left in the chest, otherwise, there is no way you will bear the smell, the scars, and rotting flesh. And that flesh can only heal with your full love and acceptance.

We each have our personal demons and stories in storage somewhere. But walking that tunnel, I know that the humidity alone will have prevented most of us from walking further.

"This journey cannot be forced, but when the time comes, you'll know and will walk without fear.
Much hesitation, but not fear."
Dr. Bak Nguyen

This is what I have established with you, over the years, an inspirational story. One that I hope can motivate and help you walk your journey, your **Quest of Identity**.

If I need to give a name to this stage, it is the **FAN** stage. But as Jonas clearly repeated time and time again, this is merely the beginning. Now that you know that a walk is waiting for you ahead, you still need the tools and the structure to equip yourself for the journey ahead. Motivation alone will not suffice.

But now, you also understand why I firmly was against forcing any of you to take that path. I am a doctor, a healer, only once you are ready to heal that I can guide you, that I can empower you. Until that awakening, I might be seen as doing more harm than good to any of you.

And this is the pledge of my Sensitive soul to all of you. I am a healer, not a guru nor a spiritual guide. That, my parents and Conformity successfully forged in me: the nobility of a doctor.

This is **ALPHA LADDERS**, Captain of your destiny.

DESTINY is not something we received,
But something we write and rewrite
Dr. BAK NGUYEN

CHAPTER 3
BIG BROTHER

by Dr. BAK NGUYEN

"We do with what we received. We copy what we see."
Dr. Bak Nguyen

I was born as my parents started fresh in a new country, on a new continent. They lost everything to war, twice! I enjoyed 3 years of exclusivity. Soon enough, my little brother came along. I loved him dearly since I had a friend to play with. Then, our little sister came 3 years later.

How I remember my childhood is that I was always the elder helping my parents. That's what they wanted out of me. Me? I was having fun with my little brother. Then, as I grew up, I inherited the pressure to give the example.

At school, I had to succeed, so my younger siblings could succeed too. At home, every time my parents wanted something done, I was the one responsible to implement it with my siblings. The reality is that my siblings were much more docile than I was.

They had an easier time at school, performed better, they were more equipped to meet my parents' expectations. I was the artist and the rebel. My parents and grandparents saw that. They loved me with all of their heart and doubled down on the **BIG BROTHER** role to keep me in line.

So from a very young age, I wasn't doing things for myself, but to give the example. The little authority they gave me was to keep me in line, to give me structure. I took care of my brother and sister as much as I could, with what I knew and what I was given. But what did I receive more? 3 years in advance. That's it!

Slowly, my brother realized that I wasn't any better than he was, so he became the new big brother to our little sister. He took over that role, freeing me for a while. He was always better equipped for that role.

A few years later, as I was accepted into dental school, my brother joined medical school instead. To my parents, I wasn't leading anything, I was lucky to be accepted. My brother was the sure bet.

Only when our little sister joined Dental school that my role as a big brother was reactivated. I paved her path and showed her everything that I knew. I had 6 years advance.

Her dream was to become a dentist. My goal was to please my parent and to survive that choice. She had all of the means to be so much better in the dental core than I was. But because I needed to lead the way, I became that dentist I thought she would become. Not out of jealousy or out of insecurity to prove a point, just out of love and responsibility.

Well, after 20 years in the profession, I am a successful dentist, one loved by his patients and one respected by his peers. I've just been honored as a **TOP 100 doctors** 2021. For someone not looking to become a doctor, that's not bad at all!

I did that because my role was to open the march, so others could follow. That's what they told me to do, because I was the eldest, I had to lead by example.

I had my share of scars and pain but I successfully triumphed for the tasks and challenges. I led the way, not just to my siblings but also to my younger cousins. That's the good side of the story. What about the other side?

Well, having not received any means or authority more than what my younger links received themselves, it was a matter of time before they all turned on me.

In times of trouble, they all look up to me for solutions and for hope. As they are successful, they do not stand near me, my presence casting a shadow too large to be avoided.

Every time something has to be done, they threw the task on me and see how I would perform. I did, cracked the code, and showed them the way. And then, I became the reminder of their moment of weakness, of doubt and insecurity.

This is a classic scenario in a large family with much to gain back from a huge loss, war and immigration. The difference was, in this case, that I was not looking for power nor to keep my authority over anyone, I was just looking to get rid of the task in hand as soon as possible, to meet the expectation of the parents, being the big brother, and to resume my dreaming and sensitivity.

The end result was the same. Much hate and jealousy came out of the equation. Those I helped the most were now my best haters. They hate me because I was always the big brother, always way ahead. I performed that role so well that it was impossible to beat me at that game. Me? I would have welcomed the relay, but no one understood that for years.

I will not be talking about them, that's not in my habits. Let's just focus on the effects it had on me. I became stronger and stronger. Being lazy and unwanting of the authority, I came to master it, always leading by example. Try telling your immigrant father that it is impossible, that's not even a possibility.

That's what I kept from my training as a big brother: nothing is ever impossible... and I do not even have much time to deliver.

Now years later, I look back on my journey, I am still the same person, one leading by example and sharing what I learned on the way. I am not inspiring my siblings or younger cousins anymore, many of them are now doctors and respected members of society. Some of them have a much higher position in the medical core that the one I hold myself. But, for some obscured reasons, they still keep the comparison with me.

I learned years ago, after much pain, to let go. I kept being who I am and move forward. Then, I found you. I now share with all of you, my experiences, perspectives, and journey. This book forced my introspection and I realized that I am still acting as the big brother leading by example. The only thing I learned from my pain is the component to let go.

"I will show you. I won't force you.
But I won't wait for you."
Dr. Bak Nguyen & William Bak

With the help of my son who was 8 by the time of that writing, I summarized who I became. With 74 books under my belt, I am pretty comfortable leading and sharing the way to those who need inspiration and guidance. I will do that with no expectation, with no burden, simply because this is who I am.

I may be famous and respected, with world records over world records, but that also brought me to the realization that I failed to grow into a great leader, failing to help the emergence of other leaders. I have grown in influence, what is next?

This was the subject of the heated conversation I had with Jonas and Brenda, two of my most trusted lieutenants and proteges. Proteges because I am their big brother showing them the way. Lieutenants because they are amongst the minds and hearts I trust to help me materialize my visions and ideas.

The main difference between them and my younger siblings and cousins is that they are answering to me, not to a third party granting me authority in time of need and revoke as soon as pride and power trips arise.

I got rid of the power trip and pride by throwing away most of the structure and hierarchy. But with those working with me on my projects, the function of each individual is very well defined, not exclusive, but defined. I always tell all of my team that I am not a boss. If I have to be a boss, that's the beginning of the end of our relationship.

I prefer to empower my team so they can surprise me with their results. I am there to give them a goal and then, empower them and help them to grow into that role they took with me. That is the structure of **Mdex & Co**, my company.

Well, the model does not fit everyone. That, I can tell you! Most required a firm hand and policy to keep moving forward. Some may not last the journey they signed up for. Some will change idea midway. Some will doubt themselves.

As a big brother, I would have stopped everything and wait for them to understand and jump back on board. But that isn't my responsibility anymore. My duty is to the mission and the vision I received from my patients, from my investors, from the team that put their faith in me. As a CEO, my mission is to deliver the promised results and to keep pushing forward.

That's where the third part of the philosophy I developed with my son William took all of its meaning: but I won't wait for you. That put the burden of results, not on my shoulders but on theirs too. I will keep showing the way with results. If you want to be part of the game, you will have to carry your own weight!

And this is where I am, as a good and gentle boss, a loved and respected doctor, and an inspiration for people looking to move forward. That's Dr. Bak. And then, I created the **ALPHAS**!

The **ALPHAS** is a community. The tag line is **WELCOME TO THE ALPHAS**. The welcoming is crucial to the brand. In other words, I give people the hope that everyone can become an Alpha.

If I keep my personal philosophy, that should be enough to write books and to inspire from a distance, but it is merely scratching the surface to really help people, to empower them to free themselves from fear. That's the promise Jonas confronted me with. How do I make that one come true?

And this is the journey of this book, **ALPHA LADDERS**. From being a big brother, I grew into a CEO. I led my young links. Today, I lead my team, and I hate to give orders. I lead showing the way. How could I show the way to you with the same intention that I had with my younger links and the results of my team members?

On that, **Mdex & Co** is one of the crown jewels of the dental industry, reinventing the economic model of delivering dentistry and how people are perceiving it.

We are also leading the coming back of the industry in **COVID** time. That isn't just me, it is the result of my teams, **TEAM MDEX**, and the **ALPHAS**. Today, I am more the spoke person than anything else. That's the success of my team members.

This is my starting point, from the legacy I received as the eldest in an immigrant family, from a trained doctor, I was and still am the Big Brother and the care giver.

"Big brother is not a status, but a role.
To keep its relevancy, one must always be ahead."
Dr. Bak Nguyen

This is **ALPHA LADDERS**, Captain of your destiny.

DESTINY is not something we received,
But something we write and rewrite
Dr. BAK NGUYEN

CHAPTER 4
WALK YOUR LEGEND

by JONAS DIOP

Do humans tend to give an image that is expected of them? I would tell you Yes in most cases, as it meets many of our basic needs as well as those of being loved and accepted, especially in a world of interaction.

We exchange goods, skills that are necessary for our survival. As we often say Man is a social animal. We are shaped by our education, our peers, our culture, habits and customs, taboos and prohibitions as well as by social pressure.

We have become masters of wearing masks, we want to please those around us, to be seen well, in the end, we conform to standards, expectations that do not come from us.

> "Tell me who is around you,
> I will tell you how you behave."
> Jonas Diop

Like Dr. Bak, some become lawyers, other doctors by social pre-determinism, they follow the path that was traced for them long before they were born.

Don't we see the children of actors becoming actors in their turn. Don't we see the children of singers becoming singers in their turn? In addition, there is great pressure on their shoulders to do much better than their predecessor in order to avoid any comparison and assert their legitimacy.

I am writing these lines to you at the age of 31 and I already know that I would not go through the famous **midlife crisis**. In this fateful age when we have a better perspective of life, many people find that they have missed theirs, allowing themselves to be fooled by the complacency of routine, caught in a hypnotic circle.

They have achieved the ambitions of others and not their own. They were constantly torn between living their dreams and a desire for security. In them is born a strong cognitive dissonance, they look at themselves in the mirror, but do not recognize themselves. They see in it a stranger and have this impression of emptiness.

Their flame flickers, should they choose between their values and their desires, by dint of frustrations, the choice is made.

"Some die inside, others do everything
to turn their flame into an inferno."
Jonas Diop

They make a 180-degree turn, try to make up for the lost time, look for each other, change their hairstyle, dress style, way of expressing themselves, and some even careers. Some even go so far as to divorce.

This, because they have denied their being, denied their desires, they have forgotten themselves.

We all have responsibilities, but they should never become a sword of Damocles. I believe there are three main goals in life:

The first: To be happy. It may sound so simple, but most people have forgotten this fact and are locking themselves into a set of rules in order to change a conscience and values that are not their own.

They always oscillate between **frustration**, **guilt**, and **judgment**. They then find themselves stuck between denying their desires and the ego of being a good person. Instead, I invite them to take my mother's advice: always be true to yourself, aligned between your values and goals, listen to your instincts.

The second: Exploit your full potential. It is the logic of human evolution, to see the world of possibilities, to surpass oneself, to achieve the impossible: from the boat to the conquest of space via the plane. As Dr. Bak says, we don't do it out of obligation, but just out of passion because it's fun.

The third: Transmit your strength of character. Once we have grasped the essence of the evolutionary process, it is natural to want to share it, we have finally reached the top of Maslow's pyramid.

Our knowledge, our mastery must leave an imprint in time so that we come closer to this **ideal of immortality**. Isn't this what Leonardo da Vinci achieved with the Mona Lisa or Genghis

Khan with his empire, they have become a part of history, their names are perpetuated generation after generation?

These last two characters had an unprecedented click. Let me tell you how it clicked with me.

I am the youngest of four siblings, which means that in the family hierarchy, I come last. Even today I am often loved as a child, the youngest one.

Especially in my mother's eyes, I will always be her baby. I had little right to speak or express my opinion on family matters.

I had to conform, follow the examples of my elders and respond to this Judeo-Christian adage from the ten commandments: Honor your father and your mother in order to have a long life on earth, that the Lord, God gives you.

In short, do not wave and be docile. My mom always encouraged me to be the best by her standards. She was waiting for me to follow a path, her path, the path of her desires, but not for me to create a new one.

The wins that I was racking up were the norm according to her, that I have 18/20 and that I being first in the class didn't matter. I had to get the highest grade, be perfect. However, I was not the horse it was put on to win the race.

Indeed, there is my big brother, taller, and favorite of my mother to whom she compared me and on whom her hopes were founded. He had more potential, to me, we were just different.

By dint of not believing in my own abilities, I just decided to do what I wanted, not out of rebellion, but just to exist, to express myself.

"Better your food with remorse than with regret."
Jonas Diop

I took my independence and was going to be recognized for my own inner geniuses. I must tell you that respect is not due to you, it must be affirmed by you.

So I was able to be on the family decision-making table the day I started to physically solve certain problems. I have become a recognized author, speaker, and business strategist.

I have helped entrepreneurs increase their turnover, people to regain self-confidence. And finally, I became a real support for my family.

I just listened to my soul longing, ended my frustration. I invite you to do so much more. To live on your terms and values. It starts as Dr. Bak said, as one will come out of his or her Quest of Identity. Walk your legend!

This is **ALPHA LADDERS**, Captain of your destiny.

DESTINY is not something we received,
But something we write and rewrite
Dr. BAK NGUYEN

CHAPTER 5

THE LAW OF ATTRACTION

by Dr. BAK NGUYEN

Being a big brother and a boss. Can we combine the two? On that, I will trust Jonas and entertain his line of thoughts. Let's address his second question: how do we find resources and leverage?

To answer this question is a little more complex. To find resource and leverage we have to break it down into 3 universal laws of physic:

- The law of Attraction
- The law of Gravity
- The law of Abundance

Only from the mastering of these 3 laws, can we find the resources to leverage as we are moving forward. Dr. Bak will tell you to have a clear vision and to state it boldly (**Attraction**), to not wait for permission and to act on your newly formed engagement (**Credibility - Gravity**), and to aim for your next win, as small as it is (**Abundance**).

This is the short version for the laziest and smartest amongst you. Now, since I promised Jonas an answer that will satisfy his curiosity and thirst, allow me to develop each of the laws.

"Leadership attracts leadership."
Christian Trudeau, former CEO founder of BCE EMERGIS

This is how my friend and mentor, Christian Trudeau opened his books with me, **HUMAN FACTOR**. The phenomenon of the **LAW OF ATTRACTION** has gained much in popularity since the last year, thanks to the book, THE SECRET.

In short, what the book says is state your desire, say it out loud and the Universe will conspire to give it to you. The first time I read that, I thought it was all crap. But then, I kept my mind open and gave it a try. You have no idea how powerful the **LAW OF ATTRACTION** can be.

When you break it down, replace the word desire with prayers and Universe with God, strike down the word conspire and you can read something very familiar: **SAY OUT LOUD YOUR PRAYERS AND GOD WILL GIVE IT TO YOU**.

The only problem with the second version is that it has been around for so long that it is not a revelation nor a secret to anyone. SECRET! That author found a way to repackage the best selling book of all times. Talk about attraction!

Her success shouldn't take away any of the wisdom and the power of the message: **CLARIFY YOUR DESIRES AND VOICE THEM UP**. If you ask me, that's is the essence of the **LAW OF ATTRACTION**. And do you know who or what it attracts? People!

State your desires, and your views clearly, boldly and people will be joining. Not the one you know on a first-name basis, those will never see beyond who you were and their own limitations. The people joining you are the ones moved by your message, of what you are looking to accomplish.

In the business world, we call that, leadership and vision. That is why I opened this answer with a quote from a leader of men who created billions in values, a man who eats and drinks like you and I; a man I look up to as a mentor and who looks at me as a friend, a young links.

The only way to forge such friendship is to attract them to you. You have no idea how the presence of Christian Trudeau in my environment and entourage, boosted my confidence and boldness to push even further my vision and audacity.

Christian is not my only mentor. On my Board of Directors, I have two other mentors of his caliber, powerful and leaders of men, Dr. Jean De Serres and Andre Chatelain. Dr. De Serres was the former president of Hema-Quebec, the equivalent of the RED CROSS and Andre Chatelain was the former number 2 of one of our big financial institutions.

To attract one man of that caliber is the chance of a lifetime. To have three of them on the same table?! Well, I must be the most fortunate of man! Together, they created and manage billions of dollars and thousands of people. Who am I to have such a chance?

"Leadership attracts leadership."
Christian Trudeau, former CEO of BCE EMERGIS

I stated my vision clearly and loudly. Then, I did not wait for permission, I started building, learning on the field, and from my mistakes.

Theirs presences around me is the confirmation that was I am doing is of importance. Their presence on my Board of Director gave my company the credibility to look for the needed resources and finance for the materialization of our vision. They are the Generals.

Before they came on board, the same recipe was very useful to recruit team members and lieutenants. The promise was then that we will give them a job and a work environment in which they can advance and accomplish themselves.

Before the team and employees, I needed to attract patients. The promise was: **FOR JOY FOR LIFE**, the tag line of Mdex. That joy was myself, as I attended to them in my dental chair. Then, my team picked up on the vibe and it became a movement. One by one, patients refer one another and Mdex became a community.

In the financial world and every day's word, Mdex is my company, but the truth is that Mdex is a community with values that I inspired. 18 years later, Mdex still evolves with these standards, but patients and team members have come to contribute with their own vision of what Mdex is.

This is what was attractive to the Generals, to my mentors: the presence of a leader and visionary empowering a community and supported by a team.

All three ingredients are crucial to the recipe: **LEADERSHIP**, **COMMUNITY**, and **TEAM**. Take one out and the formula will be imploding from its own weight.

Is short, the **LAW OF ATTRACTION** isn't about God or the Universe, but about you and the people around you. You and your desire, are the **LEADERSHIP** and **VISION**. The community and team are who you will be attracting.

It is working because since the dawn of time, this is how we've been trained, with religion, politics, and education. We are used to that format. Give the people what they want and they will follow you, at least for a while. Well, if you want the good of the people, you have a good start. Now, gather enough confidence and assurance to voice your **WILL**.

"Your WILL is not your desire, but the combination of your experience, commitment, and hunger for one thing."
Dr. Bak Nguyen

This is **ALPHA LADDERS**, Captain of your destiny.

DESTINY is not something we received,
But something we write and rewrite
Dr. BAK NGUYEN

CHAPTER 6
THE LAW OF GRAVITY

by Dr. BAK NGUYEN

Your **WILL**. That did not sound as great as we hoped, hasn't it? **WILL** is not about imposing your views upon others, but about offering who you are in the service of others. If there is one thing I learned within my 20 years as a doctor is that I am as powerful as I serve.

In other words, for as long as I am serving others, my power and influence are growing. The day that I cease that practice, I start to receive the bullets.

With my patients, that was easy. With my younger links, I was once their best ally, but I outlive my usefulness to them, so I became the reminder of their weakness... I became undesirable. And as they are stuck with their own insecurity and doubt, I keep moving forward, leaving an even bigger gap between us... and we were once so close.

My WILL was never to impose on them, but to help them, leading by example. It was still for them to walk their own path. I am walking mine. The difference is how committed each of the party are.

I am too lazy to restraint a dynamic once it has started. The laws of physic and of my own laziness will dictate that it is easier for me to speed it up than to slow down... and you know the rest of the story.

If to them, I have outlived my usefulness, to the rest of the world, I grew in credibility. As my confidence grew, I became bolder and bolder, announcing my goal in advance and achieving them, or die trying. Well, I am still alive, do the math!

With that, I have come to establish my reputation as a bold talker and an overachiever. Do you have any idea how that **GRAVITY** empowered and amplified my **POWER OF ATTRACTION**? By a triple X factor! The proof is that you are reading my words as we are.

The Law of Attraction, on its own, can be of short term and a wishful thinking to some. Combine it with the **LAW OF GRAVITY** and you are now creating a permanent movement of energy going your way.

Be warned, nothing is ever free. Everyone you are attracting will also be pressuring you, just like the Earth, Sun and the Moon interact with one another. Eventually, an equilibrium will form.

Until then, it is for you to absorb the extra energy or to compensate for the lack of tension. That's what is required of you as you are growing into a **CENTER OF GRAVITY**.

Once you've reached the status of **GRAVITY**, it is not about attraction anymore. Attraction is part of your daily. It is about managing the forces and looking for harmony before the next clash.

I wrote many times that your legend can only start the day you are out of your Quest of Identity. Well, this is what I meant. The day you are secured enough to stop looking at your belly button and your needs, you start to see the needs of the world and how you can help, that day, you are starting your legend.

With each step in that journey, your legend is growing. The irony is that for years, you get inspiration from the legends of others to finally walk yours. The day you are walking yours, you will be too busy and even blind to the sound of your own legend. When that happens, you know that you are on the right track.

If a **CENTER OF GRAVITY** is focused on its center, it will collapse. The only way for a **CENTER OF GRAVITY** to keep growing and to balance the incoming and ever-changing attractions coming his or her way is to focus on the others, not on him or herself.

And how can one grow as he focuses on others? Well, that's the easy answer. He grows with less friction and resistance since he wasn't looking at himself!

You see, as we are focus on others, our objectivity is more accurate as we are analyzing mathematically the inputs and stimuli. When one is looking at himself, well, the chances are that pride will blind most of his logic.

Think of it for a second, what is pride? Pride is to protect with all of your being something weak. Does that make any sense to you? And yet, this is our nature.

Becoming a **CENTER OF GRAVITY** and growing as one, the magic happens as you are forced to stop looking at your belly button. Trust me, those who ignored that rule aren't any more to tell you their tales.

And how do we label someone not focused on him or herself but on others? **COMPASSION**. Compassion is the key ingredient to the next law, the **LAW OF ABUNDANCE**.

If everyone can pray for more and for better, I can tell you that becoming a **CENTER OF GRAVITY** will take much more commitment, dedication, and compassion. Not passion, compassion.

"Passion is the dedication to an idea or to yourself.
Compassion is the dedication to others. And this
is not an idea, but an universal law."
Dr. Bak Nguyen

This is **ALPHA LADDERS**, Captain of your destiny.

DESTINY is not something we received,
But something we write and rewrite
Dr. BAK NGUYEN

CHAPTER 7
THE LAW OF ABUNDANCE

by Dr. BAK NGUYEN

Now the third and most attractive law of the three, the **LAW OF ABUNDANCE**. As you are attracting people and energy to you, you are growing slowly into a **CENTER OF GRAVITY**.

Once you have become a **CENTER OF GRAVITY**, just like the universe, you will be attracting more and more masses to you. Until then, it was you that were attracted by masses bigger than yourself.

The first thing to understand here is this equation is dynamic, not still. Since you are growing from the law of **ATTRACTION** to the law of **GRAVITY**, you must consider the growing part very strongly.

This means that in order to reach the **law of ABUNDANCE**, you keep growing your values, ideas, and compassion to increase the attraction you already have. This will also mean that you will have to leave your own *matrix* behind, the day you have outgrown its boundaries, if you want to keep growing.

You heard about my **YESMAN** challenge for 18 months. What do you think that was? Well, it was for me the reboot of my values since I was touching the boundaries of my belief system. What I believe in brought me that far. It will also be what will keep me still from that point on.

It took me 18 months to successfully erase the foundation of that system and to replace it with another one. Which one will you ask? Well, a few years ago, I've been awarded the Grand

Homage of the **LYS DIVERSITY**. Believe it or not, I did not know what DIVERSITY really was about. I had to google the word to write my thank you speech. That was the first stone cast.

> "Build from the differences."
> Dr. Jean De Serres, former CEO OF HEMA-QUEBEC

A few years later, this is how my friends and mentor, Dr. De Serres opened our book together, **THE RISE OF THE UNICORN**. My *former matrix* was about excellence and elitism, always trying to be the best. Or to beat the best.

Well, I have replaced those values with **FLEXIBILITY** and **COMPASSION**. The Flexibility to always reinvent the means as the needs occur and the compassion to do it, not for myself, but to serve others.

This is why you are calling me Dr. Bak. The Dr. wasn't for you, it is for me to remind myself to always keep **COMPASSION**, in other words, to care for your needs before mine. That, and to draw a smile of satisfaction on the face of my parents every time they heard the sound of the word Dr.

And the **LAW OF ABUNDANCE** in this? Well, if you've followed the logic, I've shown you the way to grow from a **DESIRE** into a **CENTER OF GRAVITY**. I just showed you how to rearrange your own *matrix* to sustain the growth of your own gravity, through flexibility and from the difference.

Think with me, as your mass is growing bigger and bigger, you are attracting more and more of the world to you. Some will be in line with your views and opinions.

The law of statistics will also dictate that most of those you attract will not be aligned with your values and belief system. Will you sort them out? Do you have any idea of the work that it will require? The greater your gravity, the bigger the sorting!

You won't survive your own growth unless your *Matrix* allows you to build from the differences with flexibility and compassion.

"Build from the differences, with FLEXIBILITY and COMPASSION. You are now holding in your hand the power of ABUNDANCE."
Dr. Bak Nguyen

With the power of **ABUNDANCE**, the needed resources are found in from of you, as you are moving forward. Most of the time, one does not even know the existence of these resources until the crucial moment.

Common wisdom will tell you to look in advance at your needs and resources and to plan accordingly. I will be the last one to tell you to cease that kind of practice. It is sounded logic and cautious preparation.

What I will urge you to keep in mind though is that you can only plan with what you know today and what you have gathered from the past. Those, if you've understood your role as a **CENTER OF GRAVITY**, are the minority of your assets. Often, with the time passing by, most of your past assets will become outdated and morphed into liabilities. From assets into liabilities, can you imagine that?

And this is crucial for you to understand. Do not misplace your sense of loyalty. You must be grateful and thankful for what you've received. But do not get attached to anything nor anyone. Those attracted to you will keep the place in your orbit, pulling their own weight.

Those sorting themselves out, let them go. You are doing both parties a huge favor. You can't attach someone to you, especially after the expiration date. In ghost stories, those coming back are never very pretty… Keep that in mind.

Back to your planning and resources. I urge you to keep your mind open to be flexible to adjust your plans and views to the incoming elements and resources. If you do not discard most of what's coming your way, use them as the resources to keep advancing.

The more open you are, the more resources you'll be attracting and keeping. And what is an overflow of resources? Abundance!

This one was straight forward!

This is **ALPHA LADDERS**, Captain of your destiny.

CHAPTER 8
CREATE YOUR OWN ABUNDANCE

by JONAS DIOP

Follow your instincts, assert your legend is easy to say, but not easy to do. What do we do when we start our life not with zero, but with an account receivable.

We are not all born equal, some come into the world with a silver spoon in their mouths, with their future laid out. Others inherite more difficult conveniences, future responsibilities: caring for a loved one, being a provider for their family this at a young age, etc.

"The universe does not expose us to a test that we cannot meet. On the contrary sometimes it tests our strength of character."

However, I am telling you, we are all born leaders, we are all born winners. We have already won the race of life: we were the first to find the solution, the gateway to developing and becoming one, when a sperm meets the egg in order to create life.

We live in a world of plenty as Dr. Bak told you, we live in a world of creation. Nowadays, we are conditioned to believe that everything is limited or even rationed. We living in a world of competition and of showing off, where one has to crush the so-called competition in order to elevate ourselves.

"A true alpha, a true leader competes with himself,
with his latent potential."
Jonas Diop

This is what I am showing you within these lines. I am delivering the best of me to you at this very moment to set the bar higher for my future self.

I attract what I desire because my state of mind is in abundance. To complement what Dr. Bak said, there are certain laws that complement the law of attraction.

The law that is the most prominent to me is the **law of proximity**. Please, let me explain. You become the average of the 5 people you hang out with the most. I have exposed it to you in other writings and I am exposing it to you again.

Dr. Bak was telling you about how his mentors managed to reshape his reality and how he reshapes theirs. It is the same to me, before knowing Dr. Bak, writing a book was to me a higher goal to be achieved since it became a step in my past, it became a step in my **personal legend**.

We are writing this one within less than 10 days, and I assure you, it's not even our fastest. You will meet various people on your way.

I invite you to create more resources, to seek wisdom and experience capable of providing you with the warmth of their advices but also to challenge you to put your hand in the fire, in order to prove yourself. With the support of a mentor, you will learn to create from nothing.

Be empathetic with people who cross your path, the ability to walk and feel in their shoes. Be kind and open to meet and exchange with mentors and peers. Have compassion at your core that will allow you to create instead of sharing the suffering of others. And what do you create, one might ask? The remedy, of course.

"Don't call on me to protest against war.
Call on me to protest for peace."
Mother Theresa

Once you have mastered the law of proximity and your emotional intelligence is high enough, you will find that in your process you have unconsciously triggered the **law of reciprocity**.

This law states that whatever we throw into the universe comes back to us ten times more. Some call it Karma. If you want to have more love, give love. If you want more money, donate money. On this last point, you are going to unblock your brain on the prejudice of **scarcity** and focus it on **abundance**.

This is how we create resources, by giving energy. Try it, for a week, smile to anyone who'll cross your path. Even without exchanging words, you will end up with so much energy that will grow yourself and your aura. Friends, opportunity, lovers, once you've grown yourself into habits, all will be attracted to you with abundance.

Spread sincere compliments and you will see that people will make your life easier just because you make them feel good around you. You are creating energy, creating your resources. Your reality is the mirror of your inner world, enrich it with a positive experience to create a more positive and virtuous circle.

"An Alpha is able to empower people around him
and make them bring out the best in them."
Jonas Diop

This is not a message of hope or even a sermon. I repeat, this is not a message of hope or a sermon. It is simply a reality!

To summarize, create your own resources by giving. The energy that you are giving will come back to you tenfold, that I can assure you. Now, you have more than you gave if you gave genuinely. And that's how one can elevate him or herself from nothing to abundance.

That's now your new reality!

I invite you to give to create, to switch to momentum mode, and enter the zone.

This is **ALPHA LADDERS**, Captain of your destiny.

DESTINY is not something we received,
But something we write and rewrite
Dr. BAK NGUYEN

CHAPTER 9

THE PRIMAL TONES
OF THE UNIVERSE

by Dr. BAK NGUYEN

It all started with your awakening. The sleeper must awake… sounds familiar? This is a theme reprised in so many classics of our culture.

One does not have to look too far to trigger his or her awakening. The voice was always there, we all know it, we each hear it every day. We simply need to tune down the noise to hear it clearly.

If you want my secret, I hear that voice very clearly either at the dawn of the day or very dark into the night. This is when the world sleeps and the noise dispersed to its thinnest. Stay up late, even better, wake up before the sun rises to listen to your inner voice, unfiltered.

As you are getting customed to listen to your inner voice, it will come easier and faster, even within the day, in the midst of the turbulence of distractions. But first, you must tune yourself to your inner voice, your inner tone.

It is very similar to playing music. We each vibrate at our unique frequency. As you can listen to your inner voice, you are opening the rest of your being to vibrate at the same frequency, yours.

When I talk about inner voice, those are not necessarily words, but an intonation, a background noise, yours. That background noise is your signature, your frequency. At first, it will feel very subtle, also imperceptible, but soon enough, as it is given space and confidence, it will grow very quickly. This is how it starts.

Actually, your whole body, as you are listening to your inner self, serves as the instrument to amplify that vibration of yours, your signature. The more you vibrate, the stronger you'll get. The stronger you'll get, the easier it will be for you to find that vibration again at any time within the day.

This may sound to you like alternative medicine or some obscure science. It is not. To all the musicians in the world, you know what I am talking about, to tune yourself with the music you are playing. Athletes call it **TO BE IN THE ZONE**. Artists call it **INSPIRATION**. Scientists refer to it as **EUREKA**.

Actually, it is all the same phenomenon, to vibrate at the same frequency of the Universe. And the Universe has many frequencies, you just need to tune into one harmoniously, effortlessly to be an instrument of power.

In the past, those with that power were referred to as instruments of God, prophets, even demons, or monsters. We often go to extremes to label what we do not understand. I don't know if there is magic in the world, but I do know the path to the universal frequencies. To listen and to tune to your inner voice is the first step.

Jonas wanted to know about **EMOTIONAL INTELLIGENCE**. Well, start vibrating your whole body to the essence of your being. As you master your own signature frequency, you can then, tune in to other frequencies.

I discovered that being in harmony and in tune with myself freed much of my capabilities. You see, most of us have been trained to look down, to look somewhere else, to ignore anything else that what we are shown and told. This is why, most of us lost our primitive tongue and language, the non-verbal.

The non-verbal language is a Universal one, as we can read different tongues, different sexes, different ages, different cultures, even different species. Yes, you read right, you can read animals using non-verbal cues.

That was our first tongue, and somehow, we forgot and lost it on the way to our evolution. Maybe standing tall and walking on two feet were not without a price. Those words may shock many of you, but deep down, you know how true this is. We all can sense it.

Well, that, that just there, what you just felt, is your inner voice. That is the same feeling that you have when you feel something is just wrong or just right, without any good reason.

"Trust your instincts, because reason and sight will always be late in the game of perception... if they aver get there."
Dr. Bak Nguyen

So **EMOTIONAL INTELLIGENCE** isn't something new to learn, it is something old to remember, to listen to. With practice, it will come back much faster than you think.

I told you that my reunification was with my wings: **CREATIVITY**, and **SENSITIVITY**. Well, gaining back my sensitivity, I had the means to listen to myself.

The more I did it, the better I got at it. I learned to tune down at will either the noise or even my own vibration. And this is where the magic happens.

Tuning down, not just the ambient noises and distraction, I also mastered the ability to tune down my own voice. Then, what I heard was the Universe. This is how I discovered the primal tones of the Universe.

Slowly I mastered the ability to empty myself and to tune in with the Universe. There are so many different frequencies and each one will lead you to a different destination, different feelings.

I got practice emptying myself as I serve my patients as a dentist. Now I am emptying myself to come in harmony with the creation, the Universe, God, give it the name you want. With all these times connecting, never finding a name to the phenomenon was of importance to the Universe or to me.

And then, I took that power of emptying myself and of listening back to our society. I gain the power of **EMPATHY**, the power to feel someone else's feeling, even from countries away. I know that it will sound weird, but I could even exert my power of **EMPATHY** with people that live in a different period.

Very hard to say if that isn't just my imagination, but I can tell you that the feeling is real. And that talking down saying that I am going crazy, well, that is an example of how we are masking our ears and hearts to our own frequency. I do not talk much about it. I just feel it.

What do you think happened in the mind of Beethoven when he was going deaf and looking to feel his music through its vibration? He was looking for a way back in tune with the Universe.

If you are still doubtful, just open a book of metaphysics. One of the bases of metaphysic is that we are not matter but energy. And energy vibrates, leaves a signature, and can be tuned up or down. Without that, we will not have electricity to light our night nor radio waves to connect.

How is it that when you feel happy, you feel the power to lift up the entire room with you? Have you ever been in the presence of the suffering of someone else that took away the colors of your sight for a little while? We have all experienced such a phenomenon, but yet, we are trained to ignore them. Well, stop ignoring what is around you, starting with yourself.

You want a way to trigger your **EMOTIONAL INTELLIGENCE?** Listen to yourself daily, Do it at the dawn of the day, meditating, writing, painting, playing music. Do something that does not involve the entry of an exterior source of information.

Reading will not get you to listen to yourself nor the Universe. Listening to music might prep your mind, but might also tune you to the music instead of your frequency. You need a moment without distraction.

And where that will lead you to? Well, in my case, it led me to write world records upon world records, discovering more and more of the powers of the Universe.

I won't lie to you. At the dawn of my day, I listen to myself. As I feel the harmony with a primal tones of the Universe, I sit down in front of my laptop and start writing. I lock myself in that frequency listening to movies' soundtracks.

To me, that is not a distraction, but an anchor to reconnect where I last left it. But before one can polarize the power of the Universe and anchor it, one must start to listen to his or her inner voice first.

Then, learn to tune up and down the ambient noise and the inner voice. Well, I do not see the advantage to tune up the ambient noise, but to focus on one tread and to amplify it, that's **EMPATHY**.

Another way to access such harmony that I found is to play music, at any time of the day. Playing music, to really play, is not to repeat time and time again the same note to perfection but to vibrate at the frequency of the artists who either composed the song or those interpreting it.

For that, you must first empty yourself and be available to listen. Literally, to listen. Then, feel the vibration and the message of the notes. Sometimes the messages are words, but very often, it is not verbal cues. Music, everyone understands, we can all enjoy music and feel how it affects our mood.

Well, the signature of that music is the emotion of the song. Sad, happy, anxious, we can all pick up on the human emotions transmitted within that songs. If we have emptied ourselves and we are available, very soon that emotion will fill our heart and we will be an instrument of its expression.

This is the exact way to vibrate, to tune down, and to tune in. Practice playing music and feel yourself vibrating.

"Emotions are the signatures of a moment."
Dr. Bak Nguyen

Vibrating the emotion imprinted in a song will have you experience what the original artist experienced at its conception. That's **EMPATHY**. Now, try without music, focusing on someone. It will come. You will start to feel what it feels like to be in someone else's shoes.

Use the power of **EMOTIONS** to discover yourself. In other words, if you allow yourself to vibrate fully your emotions, privately, you are discovering the moments that defined you, the truth about your past and preference, not the narrative you kept.

Once you have made peace with your narrative, you have learned to tune down most of the noise obstructing your perception of the exterior world. Once you have experienced the vibration of yourself enough times, you will feel secure enough to even tune that frequency down.

As a comparison, if you leave in the city, you may look up at the sky at night, there is just some much your eyes can see, even on a clear night. Just step out of the city, 30 miles away will suffice. Now, look up at night and see all the stars you missed. And stars are suns, how can we miss a sun, left alone, suns?

Well, do not underestimate the power of the noise and its impairment of your perception of the Universe, of the world, of people, of events.

Experience the whole scope of your emotions to gain confidence. And as you are ready, tune to that frequency you have identified as your way down to experience the vastness of the Universe. The feeling is one of magnitude and a nurturing one. If one wanted to fly, this is even more exhilarating.

From these powers, I read the world, the people, and the events. I can vibrate at someone else frequency to feel what that person is feeling. This is also how I came to become such a loved doctor because I am accompanying my patients through their treatments and surgeries. I am not only the hands healing them, I lend them my soul to heal too.

Doing that daily, doing that again and again, I do not feel threaten to vibrating at any frequency, even the negative ones. Negative frequencies are often an expression of a deep suffering. Even those can be untied and freed.

What I did for the last two decades was to change the world a smile at a time. I did that being a healer, available to one soul at a time. Now that I discovered the immense powers from my **EMOTIONS**, I am healing the world, a soul at a time, with a different medium, writing.

I am healing the world because it has grown part of my nature, the doctor title. But my real power and impact are when I vibrate at the frequencies of the Universe and I create. This chapter is an example of it.

Writing, the chapter that I had in mind about **EMOTIONAL INTELLIGENCE** was by far a different one than the one you just read. One must less interesting and down to Earth. I emptied myself and make myself available to vibrate. And this is how I grow.

"A mind that vibrates to a higher energy
will never come back at its original level."
Albert Einstein

This is **ALPHA LADDERS**, Captain of your destiny.

DESTINY is not something we received,
But something we write and rewrite
Dr. BAK NGUYEN

CHAPTER 10
LIVING FOREVER

by Dr. BAK NGUYEN

Emptying myself daily and tuning in with the frequencies of my emotions and then, of the Universe, I discovered powers. Playing the piano became the main gauge of the progression of my intelligence, emotional intelligence.

What I have to practice at the beginning, now I simply enjoy, playing along.

> "I stop trying to duplicate what I hear,
> I simply danced along."
> Dr. Bak Nguyen

It was fun and very pleasant. So I did it times and times again, discovering new songs and new styles, and becoming better and better at it. I finally successfully tuned in to Jazz lately. That's a personal victory since Jazz always eluded me.

Before, there were musics I liked and musics I didn't. Well, today, I still have my preferences but I can play anything and I will empower the room by matching the tastes of my guesses.

Before I will have considered such actions spineless or something close to intellectual prostitution. Looking back, I could see how insecure and mediocre I was.

Today, I welcome the experience and will make all of my being available to empower the emotion and the moment, playing that particular music. It is not with the music that I am merging, but with the vibe of my guesses. I play and I learn.

What amazed me the most is that I am doing most of this effortlessly, without any practice, and having so much fun enjoying myself. Well, that was the materialization of the tones of music, one of the primal tones of the Universe accessible to me.

I wrote about music in many of my books, of how it empowers me to my soul and to the Universe. It is the first time that the process is broken down to this level. If you want to follow these footsteps, you will have to do more than to read these lines, you will have to sit down and to pick up an instrument too.

This isn't the only way, but an accessible one to all of you who have any experience with music and skills with any instruments. To you, I say enjoy your moments, surf your emotions until you feel tall, and secure enough to free them, all of them.

"Freeing your emotions is how one empties him
or herself to vibrate at a higher frequency."
Dr. Bak Nguyen

Musicians, elevate yourself and the world with you. This is nothing new, but you know that through the means of music, you live forever. That piece of your soul vibrating will last for as long as people will be tuning in. Now the question is: How many times will you live forever?

You do not play music, that's fine. Can you dance? Do you paint? Can you write? I am not an expert in the other fields, but writing, that I know.

Writing is a little more complex than playing music since you have no templates (songs) to follow nor no one to ease your way in (band, orchestra, fellow musicians). When you write, you are confronted with yourself and yourself alone. It is a powerful means to the vastness of the Universe, but one that will take much more mastering on your part.

To be honest, I started music long before I start writing. I told you that I usually wake up before the dawn of the day without any alarm. I listen to the silence and to the tones. Sometimes it is my inner tone, but more and more often, it is now the tone available, those of the Universe, and sometimes, the tone of other people.

This is what I am doing as I invite someone to join in to co-author a book with me. We mingle intellectually, creating a space and vibe unique to the interaction of our souls. I can tell you that those who are doing the exercise with me, there is nothing one can hide. You now have direct access to the heart and soul of someone.

This is no manipulation of any kind, the connection goes both ways. Everything is open and on the table to the other to see. Just like in a poker game, the only question is where does the other person looking, is it at his own cards or at the rest of the table. That the communion and synergy as I co-write with someone.

Just like playing music, I came to grow confident enough to mingle with anyone, even a stranger. Within the next hours and days, I will know and feel the core of that person. Most of the time, we are having a great time surfing each other's vibes. Often, I elevate their vibe to a higher frequency as I am more familiar with the exercise.

Some other times, well, the soul I touched isn't one that I would like to keep a connection with. Just like playing music, that was just a book, a moment, a diversity in the scope of the possibilities. I finish the song and I move on.

I can tell you that before reaching such stage, one must be very secure with him or herself. We are all influenced by the people and events we come in contact with, that's the nature of a frequency. Some will add up, some will just compete for the same spot, and some will be canceling your frequency.

But your frequency is not like a fire that can go extinct. Your frequency is the sum of the vibration of your being. For as long as you are alive, you are vibrating.

It is not because you have vibrated at a certain level that you are contaminated. Sure, you will never go back to what you were before, but wasn't that the purpose of Life, to grow, to experiment?

It is not because you tuned down your frequency to the bare minimum that you will die. All you will have done is to experience something different, something new. This is the insurance that I would like you to achieve.

"Confidence is sexy."
Dr. Bak Nguyen

That's my favorite quote and it summarizes perfectly the state of mind of one emptying him or herself to grow in the vastness of the Canvas, the Universe. Confidence is key.

Some lucky are born confident. But as a general rule, confidence is built and nurtured. You can break or make confidence. This is hope and danger all in one. I was born confident. Then, I got tested to my core as Conformity melted my natural confidence into its mold. I survive and thrive, but it was very painful.

I do not wish that to anyone. It was cruel, even with the best of intentions. It was not efficient since most of the forged values are quickly fading away with my awakening. And it is sometimes and consuming and energy-hungry.

The alternative is to let the heart experience freely its emotions, dancing, singing, and crying without holding any tears in. Can you feel how good that makes you feel? You feel… alive!

Each time, there wasn't any consumption of energy, on the contrary, that person feeling was radiating energy. Why do we like to listen to music and stories? Because it stimulates us at our cores.

And it is so fun to surf such feelings. So what does that person do? He or she will just dive back in, again and again, swimming like a dolphin in the waves of the scope of human emotions and the tones of the Universe. Because it was pleasant and fun, it was effortless, frictionless. I don't know about you, but to me, frictionless is the most effective way, one without any loss.

"I am just a lazy guy looking for fun."
Dr. Bak Nguyen

Now you understand my thoughts and essence. I write to share with you as I discover and surf the waves of the Universe. That's the great part of the story. For those of you who would like to follow in my footsteps writing, here are some pointers.

Get rid of your first book as soon as possible. In that first book, it is impossible for you to be tuned in at any but yourself, trying to look perfect. Do not feel bad, it is your birth, it is about you, it has to be.

Everyone has a story and everyone is somehow born. That's boring. What are you doing from that point on is what may hold the key to an interesting story, your legend.

Get rid of your first book and then, feel the satisfaction building up your confidence. Let that confidence grow enough to let go. Now, try now writing about something else than yourself, but use all of your being to make these words alive. Do not just write them, feel them, sing them, and listen to their vibration. Only then, write them so they can be shared forever.

That communion you just felt is your soul imprinting a moment crystallized within a jewel: a song, a poem, a story. If the song, poem, or story was about you, you have limited the interests to its bare minimum.

If the song, poem, or story uses you as an example to paint a universal emotion, well you just start living forever. Your body will cease one day, but your frequency will prevail. And that is done without any trauma, any violence nor pain just fun and the full enjoyment of the moment. That's efficient!

Those are the two paths I know to eternal life, to the tones of the Universe. I am sure that there are many, many more. Feel free to explore and to find your own. The easiest way to keep your quest going is to share back.

> "Only by sharing, you are leaving
> imprints of your frequency."
> Dr. Bak Nguyen

Didn't you want to live forever? Well, I wrote many times now that "Sharing is the way to grow." Today, I realize how true that quote is, but how of an understatement it also is. You should be reading:

> "Share to live forever!"
> Dr. Bak Nguyen

This is **ALPHA LADDERS**, Captain of your destiny.

> DESTINY is not something we received,
> **But something we write and rewrite**
> Dr. BAK NGUYEN

CHAPTER 11
THE GLASS AND THE WINE

by Dr. BAK NGUYEN

I realized that the last chapter was very dense and that I left most of you mesmerized. A conversation with William pointed that out. In this chapter, I will duplicate the conversation I had with my 10 years old son so he understands the concept of living forever.

EMOTIONS

First, we have to establish what is a feeling. A feeling is something you feel vibrating inside of you. Your whole body is reacting to that feeling. You can repress it, you can let it be, either way, you felt that something inside of you changed. You clicked, to use Jonas' wording.

An emotion is not something you can touch, see, hear, or smell, but you know how real it can be. And that vibration that you felt, well, it awoke all of you being to feel **alive**.

VIBRATION

Secondly, we need to establish the concept of vibration and how it is amplified. The easiest example that comes to my mind is to have an emptied glass of wine. Fill it completely with water.

Then, dip your finger in that water and move your wet finger around the edge of that glass. You will hear a sound. That's the amplification of the vibration that you are causing.

Now, empty a quart of the glass. The glass is now only 3 quarters full. Move your finger again on its edge. The sound you are hearing is louder and higher.

Empty half of the glass. The sound is even louder and of a higher pitch (frequency). I'll let you run your own experiment. The fullest the glass, the weaker (the volume) and lower the sound it produces. The emptier the glass, the higher and louder the sound.

This helps establish that concept of vibration and emptiness to empower.

FEELING

When you are feeling, you are vibrating. You are the glass and emotions, events or people are the finger moving on your edge. The fullest you are, the lowest and weak will be the sound coming out. The more available you are (empty), the more the sound coming out will be loud and of a higher frequency.

You see, emotions, events, and people are not the frequencies. They are the triggers to you, as a musical instrument, to voice.

What you make of that trigger, how it resonates, and what message will be perceived is depending on how available you were as you voiced up that trigger.

FREQUENCIES

There are no good or bad frequencies, there are just frequencies. In metaphysics, psychology, and medicine, it has been clearly established that the happier a person is, the higher his or her frequency. It is the same with the healthier as person is.

The voices of children are also of a higher pitch. It has well been recognized that that tone is stimulating positively the ears, especially of children.

Well, that is not completely true, at a certain level, a too high frequency will be uncomfortable and might hurt the ear. Let say that within the normal range of perceivable sound, before reaching the extremes, which are never comfortable things, the higher the frequency, the more joyful it will be perceived.

And how about people with a low bass voice? Until now, we were addressing the level of energy and talking about joy. A lower frequency does not mean bad, but different. Usually, a person with a lower tone of voice can be perceived as reassuring, lowering the stress in the air. Care for the wording here, lowering the stress, the available energy in the air.

Again, that will depend on the message conveyed, and its intentions, but you got the picture. Strictly physic based, the higher a frequency without the normal range, the happier and healthier the result of the vibration.

And how can we obtain a higher frequency from a glass? When it is empty, not full. This established the concept of emptying yourself to be available to the Universe.

CONTAMINATION

To use the analogy of the glass, can it be refilled after being emptied? Absolutely. Can it be purged once filled? Absolutely. Actually, the best way to refill a glass of wine, is to clean it before having a fresh refill. Everyone can understand the imagery.

Well, do I have to say more about ourselves? Since we only have one glass, we use and reuse it again and again. How does it taste if you never emptied it completely to clean it? Let say that they were important things to you. As you are pouring new wine, or new water, in the glass, it is mixing up with what was there.

It might taste different, but eventually, everything will share the same aftertaste. This is why it is so important to clean, crystal clear, your glass. This is why it is so important to empty yourself often.

Let's continue with the glass and wine analogy. Will you throw away a half bottle? Maybe, but that bottle was surely a cheap bottle of wine. So if you are having a wine that is worth your while, logic will dictate that you will use a clean glass to enjoy the newly open bottle of wine, and that you will enjoy finishing that bottle that evening.

Think of the glass as yourself and the wine as your emotions. Well, no emotions are cheap, that, I can tell you! So the best practice is to feel your emotions is within the same evening, fill up that crystal clear glass, and let go of your emotions.

As the glass is full at first, the energy and frequency will be lower. Sometimes shy, sometimes low. But as you drink that glass and it is emptying, the frequency will be higher and more resonant, exactly as the glass of water singing under your finger.

Just like the best bottle of wine, spend the rest of the evening on it. The frequency will get higher and higher. And as you have let it express itself to its apogee, you can now let it go. You will be feeling lighter and very alive doing so.

And how does a good bottle of wine taste a few days after you've started it? Well, if you do not enjoy within the next few days, it will turn into vinegar. It is the same with your emotions. Express fully your emotions and don't save for later, it won't get any better.

After the night, clean your glass and have it ready to drink water, milk, or coffee in the morning. Do so in a clean glass. You do that for your own pleasure, for your own good, for your own health.

If you've emptied your glass completely and that you have cleaned it accordingly, well, whatever you drank yesterday will not affect the taste of what you will be drinking today... unless you have leftover and residual staining your crystal glass and aftertaste.

I think that now, you have a crystal clear image.

LIVING FOREVER

So we have established the GLASS, the vibration, and the pitch of the frequencies (from HIGH to LOW). Well, using music as an example, playing or singing a song, we are the instruments replicating the vibration contained and intended.

The more available we are, the better we will express that vibration imprinted in that song, poem, or book. And as we do so, we are mingling with the original vibration of its creators. Somehow, we have established a connection, for a moment, with a frequency that was generated long ago.

Frequencies aren't subjected to time and space as we are. Matter is subjected to time and space, not energy. Do I have to remind you that we are energy, not matter? We are alive, aren't we?

Enjoying a song, a poem, a book, we are connecting. The role can also be reversed. If we are the ones writing, composing, painting or singing, that part of us vibrating in the moment can travel through time and space until someone else will vibrate to our frequency again.

If we are energy, this is how we can live forever, for as long as what we shared is still of interest to someone else. But do so with in a crystal clear and empty glass to begin with, the reading and the composing, because *what we do will echo for eternity**.

This is **ALPHA LADDERS**, Captain of your destiny.

DESTINY is not something we received,
But something we write and rewrite
Dr. BAK NGUYEN

* A quote borrowed from the movie GLADIATOR by directed by Ridley Scott and written by David Franzoni, John Logan, and William Nicholson.

CHAPTER 12
AKA TORNADO

by Dr. BAK NGUYEN

Things did not happen overnight, but within the years following. After my reunification with my wings, I turned down the possibility to run for office to spend more and more time with my piano.

I have to say that around that time, I haven't touched a piano for 15 years… and I bought a YAMAHA grand piano to display in my banking hall. This is how I call my living room.

At first, I was intimidated by the piano. Then, slowly, I played and played more. I add a Bose speaker linked with my iPad pro and download musical apps allowing me to play along with a band. That added the fun to my reunification process, especially that now I had to learn to walk and talk being whole, finding synergy between my logic and creativity, between my boldness and sensitivity.

I played and healed improving my musical skills. I did not run for office, and I was so happy. I was whole. Amongst the last task Mohamed asked me to do as my coach, was to take the Gallup Institute test to measure intelligence. I did so very reluctantly, I hate tests.

But since I broke the man's heart, not running for office, I took the test as a sign of friendship and gratitude to the man who opened the door to my reunification.

Contrary to the IQ test, the **Gallup Institute** developed another kind of test, one measuring the different kinds of intelligence one has. There are 34 different kinds of intelligence (talents) mapped by the Gallup Institute. According to the Gallup Institute, people usually score 5 different kinds of intelligence. Some gifted people will be scoring up to 8.

Well, I took the test twice and I scored 20 kinds! 19 the first time and 21 the second time. I thought that it was a mistake, but after research, I realized the seriousness of the work of the Institute. I shared my discovery with Mohamed. A light went through his eye. Very quickly, what appears as joy changed into regrets.

I noticed and felt his regrets with my newly discovered power of empathy. We did talk, but about the weather, family, and vacations. I was left by myself to understand what that meant.

Well, after a good night's sleep, I woke up with the answer imprinted on my forehead: I was a **HYBRID**. Nature gifted me with 8 talents, from which sensitivity and creativity were the most prominent.

Then, my parents and Conformity melt my essence to shape a doctor out of me. I survived the process and thrived, meeting those standards of logic and perfection. I inherited 8 more talents.

That brings our count to 16. How do you explain the 4 extra strengths? Well, even if my reunification is new, I had to live with myself for all these years. In chemistry, there is a known concept that when you add 2 ingredients together, the result is not the sum of the attributes of each ingredient.

Sometimes the end result will have more attributes, other times, less. And often, the attributes aren't the same that added up either. Well, the concept of synergy is that one ingredient will trigger the other one and explode its potential.

That's what happened with me and my 2 natures, one given by nature and the other one inherited as a legacy. Those two had to coexist, even without me fully aware of the phenomenon. So they interacted with one another.

In my case, synergy has resulted out of the equation, adding up both of the 8 kinds of intelligence from each part of myself, plus 4 more emerged from the interaction of them. Flexibility was the predominant intelligence from the synergy.

That explains a lot. But it was also much to take in. Not having all of the answers and not understanding all of their meaning, I keep playing the piano to empty myself and to merge with other frequencies. Until I started an online challenge.

For a summer, I swam every day 20 laps and posted proof of that on my social media. I was looking to find a remedy to my weight problem. I did not lose a single pound, but I did post every day for a whole summer, 20 laps minimum each day, no matter the weather.

I must say that I was surprised by my consistency. Then, as the Fall arrived, it was too cold for me to keep swimming. I pushed it until late September, but I had to eventually close the pool for the cold season arriving.

Then, with the help of my personal trainer, coach Dino Masson, I transferred that momentum into writing. Instead of posting a picture of me finishing 20 laps a day, I started posting a chapter written a day, sometimes, 2.

For the whole story about the secret of **MOMENTUM**, I will refer you to my 7th book written with coach Dino Masson, **MOMENTUM TRANSFER**. But in short, we found a way to transfer the energy doing physical activity into a creative momentum writing books. You know the rest of the story...

In that book, I talk about the **EYE** of the **TORNADO**, a place of serenity. I felt it, I experienced it, but never it has been as clear to me until I wrote this book: the passage about emptying up.

The **EYE** of the **TORNADO** is serenity because it is the absolute absence. I successfully emptied myself to the point that I created attraction toward that void. I was growing more and more into a **CENTER OF GRAVITY** and my center was emptiness, this is why I could grow as fast and as much.

Physic will usually explain the creation of a tornado from the meeting of 2 opposite forces interacting together: a mass of hot air and a mass of colder air. Well, in my case, I was creating a tornado from thin air. I did so using emptiness. And becoming better and better at emptying myself, I could grow a tornado within minutes, from literally nothing.

That explains much of what happened next. Everyone crossing my path will tell you one of the two followings:

- I am a kind person, amongst the gentler that they have come to meet.
- I am a force of Nature, do not stand in my way.

For reference, the latest person stating me as **KINDNESS** is **ALPHA FOUNDING MEMBER**, Dr. Paul Ouellette, one of the veterans of modern orthodontics. His exact word was **COMPASSION**.

Dr. Jean De Serres was amongst the first people to publicly refer to me as a **FORCE OF NATURE** in the preface he wrote for my first book, **SYMPHONY OF SKILLS**.

I am sharing the stories that I know because I exchanged and shared with both Paul and Jean. But google my name and read the reviews, you will see that what I am citing in here are facts, not opinions.

I was very well trained by Conformity in the art of **HEALING** and by Mohamed in the art of **POWER & INFLUENCE**. I am kind and compassionate, but as the needs occur, I will be a force for change, one to be reckoned with.

Years later, I will write a whole book about the discovering of my powers and how I learned to master them for the service of a better world. That book is titled **TORNADO**.

Well, the idea of bringing all of it back into this journey is to retrace my footsteps and to breakdown the mindsets and emotions that built Dr. Bak as you know him today: a kind force of Nature.

Actually, I became that powerful because I was open to meet with more and more people. Because I was kind enough to empower those I meet and to vibrate at their frequency. Every time, I helped them to their goals. Me? I was learning and growing doing so.

From a doctor with the power of healing, I became an inspiration and a motivator with the power to empower and the power of hope. Again, if you stop and think about my process, it now makes so much sense. I grew more and more powerful because I was serving more and more people.

I serve more and more people because, at my core, I am kind enough to empty myself to be available to them. Just like that glass of wine, I vibrated at a higher and higher frequency, helping people to heal with hope, and empowering the dreamers and drivers to impact the world with their achievements. This is how **Mdex** is such a success. This is how the **ALPHAS** were born.

"With a confident and gentle core, empty to be available,
this is how I became the legend of Dr. Bak,
AKA the Tornado."

Dr. Bak Nguyen

Today, I am writing books at a world record pace. I am still the CEO of a dental company with the potential to change the world for the better. I am still servicing my patients, a smile at a time as a respected and, above all, a loved dentist. I am doing that while my teams are preparing my entrance back to Hollywood with a series of documentaries.

Another division, led by Jonas Diop is structuring my thoughts and influences into a community, **THE ALPHAS**, and the creation of **ALPHA CLASS**, books, seminars, and motivational events. And this is on top of all the projects that I am not authorized to disclose due to Non-Disclosure Agreements, a standard in the financial world.

But this journey is not about me. I am an example to help you understand that it is possible. Everything you are reading from me, you can research and find proofs and facts. Those are the traces that I leave.

That was my story of the last years. Now, I want more, much more. I want to grow from a winner into a great leader. And for that, I need your help. Actually, to become a great leader, I need to help you to find your powers and to grow into champions and leaders yourself.

I need to do so without slowing down my pace nor diverging from my core mission. That's the intent of this book, this journey.

You too will walk your Quest of Identity and will go through your tunnel. You too will find your chest. What you will find in it is what you left behind. You know pretty well what you left behind, even if you have long forgotten about it.

My story is entertaining you. My journey is giving you the hope that it is accessible and within reach. Now, as promised, I will show you. I won't force you. It is for you to make up your mind and to walk the day you feel ready. And that day will come, sooner or later.

"To each our own pace."
Dr. Bak Nguyen

It took me nearly 40 years to understand what and who I am. Even with the reputation of a sprinter and a tornado, my second birth will have taken so much time to occur. And I am at peace with it. I am today whole and happy.

Not satisfied, but happy. I will be satisfied the day I am no more. And then, you will revive my essence vibrating my frequency reading my books. And you'll be doing so, not for me, but for you.

That's the essence of the tornado, to empty yourself and have nothing at your core. That's the only way to be available and to vibe at the different frequencies of the Universe. Do you still want to grow?

"Share to live forever."
Dr. Bak Nguyen

This is **ALPHA LADDERS**, Captain of your destiny.

DESTINY is not something we received,
But something we write and rewrite
Dr. BAK NGUYEN

CHAPTER 13
REBOOT

by Dr. BAK NGUYEN

In the last chapter, I started by telling you that the awakening, the reunification, and the transformation took years to materialize, transforming me from a product of Conformity into a force of Nature.

Well, it took years but also much dedication. In the Glass analogy, we have to empty our glass and also to clean it. I was trying my best to empty mine, successfully, but somehow the aftertaste was still the same. I needed **a way to clean**, even to sterilize my glass. I found that solution in a total reboot of my system of values.

I've been raised in the belief system of perfection and elitism. Well, that got me so far. I could empty my emotions, empty my environment but if I keep the same **sorting system**, I will repopulate my environment with the same people, generating the same emotions. I was facing a dead-end. Until one word appeared in my mind: **YES**.

I needed a reboot of my values and beliefs system. I also knew that some of my old systems will need to be upgraded or completely replaced. But which one and with what? If I keep the same system of sorting, I might end up doing all of this purge for nothing! So I got rid of the sorting system too.

Me the elite, trained to be or to beat the best, always looking to be amongst the best and evolving only with those with the same values… I threw that away.

I decided to say **YES** to literally every proposal to taste the diversity of the world. The only restriction was the financial decisions, those I gave all of my power to the person I most trusted, my best friend, business partner, and wife, Tranie Vo.

Besides the financial decisions, I was free to try everything with anyone. Well, that nearly brought me to divorce as I was flirting with fire and passion… but I survived and learned from that too.

For the complete story of my **YESMAN** challenge of 18 months, I will refer you to the series of books titled **THE POWER OF YES**. For the story around my midlife crisis and the edge of what could have been my divorce, **REBOOT** is the book you want to look for.

Here, I will summarize 18 months of **REBOOTING**, mingling with people from every horizon, some good, some great, and some, simply bad. I did not care, I did not judge, I mingled and I learned to see the real face of everyone.

In the past, such a journey will have repulsed me, thinking that I will be losing my time and risking contamination. I was thinking that because I was insecure and because I did not clean my Glass daily.

During my 18 months challenge, I emptied up and was available to vibrate at the frequency offered to me. I took the first one available. I tried all of the frequencies offered to me.

And I vibed those experiences and emotions to their full extent.

But at the end of the day, I also keep a very safe habit to clean my glass crystal clear. That was the secret ingredient. In my case, writing about my experiences and emotions was my way to vibrate the frequencies to their Apogee and to let them go.

Romance, friendship, brotherhood, treason, abuse, I was living in a live soap opera. What help is that I am a man of respect and one of great taste, I did not cross any line that I would have to bear the regrets.

Saying **YES** to everything did not mean that there were no limits anymore. It simply meant that I was giving myself the luxury to weigh the question and its possibilities.

Swimming that environment for 18 months and verbally open about my challenges on interviews, on radio, on stage attracted many, many interesting adventures and propositions. The introductions of each of my books serve as my diary for what happened in between each of the titles.

All of these introductions and conclusions were also repackaged into the franchise of books titled **THE POWER OF YES**. You should have a much in-depth vision of how it was to be Dr. Bak rebooting going through that franchise of books.

That being said, what I learned and mastered from that experience is today one of my principal attributes and strengths: the power of **OPENNESS** and of **FLEXIBILITY**.

Open yourself to the world! Then, you receive much of the world going your way. You are also open so anyone could come and read you like a book.

"There is no protection from openness. You open yourself to vulnerability and well as to enriching experiences."
Dr. Bak Nguyen

From there, I gained much confidence, mingling with the diversity of values, of thoughts, of position, of everything. I mingled, but I never forget to empty and to clean my glass too, almost religiously at every dawn of the day.

This is really how I came up with my signature phrase: **CONFIDENCE IS SEXY.** It really is! You have no idea how my appeal went to the roof as I stopped trying to be better, to be someone I was not.

On that, here is a very funny anecdote. At the birthday of my wife that year, I got invited to appear in a conference for women at the Saint-Joseph Basilica in Montreal. I was not inclined to accept but my host knew about my **YESMAN** challenge. He played to me my own words to force my hand.

Well, I ended up in front of an audience of women. I did not prepare any speech, and I was announced as an inspirational leader. Well, on stage, I took the microphone and share with them a secret: how I boost my charisma.

The room went silent, they were drinking my words. Well, I told them what I will repeat to you today, I became very charming the day I cease to project myself as James Bond. Don't laugh at me, every man, at some point in their lives, aspire to be James Bond.

But if I am not James Bond, who am I? I wondered. Well, I looked in the mirror and the closest character I could see looking back at me was Shrek! That made the entire room cry, so much they were laughing.

Well, that was no joke. I really stop trying to be James Bond and accepted myself as Shrek. True story, from that day on, my popularity and appeal, not only sex appeal but appeal went through the roof! How? Thanks to confidence!

"Confidence is sexy."
Dr. Bak Nguyen

I don't remember what the rest of the talk was about, but the audience did not care either, they were in love with me from that moment. And people talk.

From one event to the next, I was invited to interviews, on radio shows, to give seminars. For 18 months, I accepted every single invitation.

Before I was known as the elite and a little snobby and arrogant. I was still the same person but now, I embrace the opportunity and the day with **YES** first. Well, my reputation grew to accessible, humble, and a very, very interesting personality.

And above all, what people loved the most about my appearance was that I wasn't playing a character, I was myself, living and rebooting in front of them.

I must say that I grew a big fan base from my 18 months challenge. Who are they? And where are they? Well, I don't know. I never really understood what I've become. It was my entourage that keeps saying that I had a huge base of followers.

I refused to believe their flatteries until I could not walk downtown Montreal and not be greeted by a stranger, man and woman, smiling at me.

At first, they were women smiling at me. I must say that I enjoyed the attention. Some even ask to have selfies with me. They all said that they were fans. Some were gorgeous... I did not know what to believe.

With women, that was surely very flattering. And then, men came too! Some even approached me and asked to shake my hand. I wasn't sure about his intentions. He told me that I was the LinkedIn celebrity writing books with his son! I couldn't refuse to shake his hand. Then, we exchange business cards. He was the vice-president of a financial firm. And that kind of story repeats itself weekly.

Before COVID, every time I walked in downtown Montreal, I had a new story to share. Now in COVID time, I received those from the social media and through emails... those I have to sort out the fans from those trying to sell me something. But the fans are really there.

Curiously enough, I was too into scoring my next win, to let my newly found celebrity go to my head. I remained the same man, one open and willing to take on the next adventure. I became Dr. Bak.

18 months later, I celebrated the end of my challenge and reboot on stage, in front of an audience of 300 plus people as the anchor of the **POWER OF YES**.

To empty myself and to clean my **glass crystal clear**, I dive into diversity and came out a different man. Saying **YES** to everything and writing about my emotions and experiences rebooted me completely.

I had the power of **EMPATHY** and of **TORNADO** before. Now, combined with the power of **OPENNESS** and of **CONFIDENCE** and you have a **CENTER OF GRAVITY**, a huge one.

It has been 40 months since I first started my **YESMAN** challenge. Even though I am not doing the **YESMAN** challenge anymore, I am not resuming to my old self. I have become a **YESMAN**, one with ideas, impact, and influence.

If you wanted the blueprint of my powers and how I grew them, I just gave you my complete journey. Maybe not complete with all the little details, but you got the main narrative. For more details, please refer to the franchise of book named **THE POWER OF YES** available on Amazon, Barnes & Noble, and of course, Apple Books.

There are discussions about making them also available into Audio format **U.A.X.** (Ultimate Audio Experience), streaming on Spotify and Apple Music. But that isn't done yet. And you know me, I am a **YESMAN**...

> "All good things start with a YES."
> Dr. Bak Nguyen

This is how I rebooted myself and boosted my inner powers to become superpowers. The Gallup test was took before my **YESMAN** challenge. Can you imagine what would be my score now? I wonder too!

This is **ALPHA LADDERS**, Captain of your destiny.

DESTINY is not something we received,
But something we write and rewrite
Dr. BAK NGUYEN

CHAPTER 14

LEARN TO UNLEARN IN ORDER TO FINALLY KNOW

by JONAS DIOP

"Through this book, I get even
closer to immortality!"
Jonas Diop

This testament, I bequeath it not only to my future children but also to the generations which will succeed me. It is my duty to synthesize the paths to success so that they can be useful to as many people as possible.

"We grow through sharing."
Jonas Diop

By doing this meticulous work of searching for answers, I am doing it as much for you as I am doing it for myself. I evolve, I raise my vibrational frequency, I create energy.

How to grow confidence? Where to find the resources? What triggers leadership?

We have opened the door to answers to these existential questions. Brenda in the next tome will bring you her insight and understanding of the process of amplifying your own geniuses.

Yes, you do have a geniuses. You can express it through what is called your talents, or even your sharing of advice, your way of acting.

If you doubt your geniuses, just take the dive and experiment to produce, to have a result. As Dr. Bak says: It may not be the best result, but it is way beyond nothing, gain confidence, and build on it.

He had taken the painter's allegory to remind me of it. An artist will first make a sketch, then gradually add touches of paint, which will make the first layer, then the second until reaching a masterpiece.

I had ignored this fundamental rule for my own book: Now or never. I wrote it the first time, then re-read it and deleted it. I wrote it a second time then re-read it and erased it again. A third time, and for this one, Dr. Bak told me not to erase any more.

So after more than 2 years and a month of the release of this book, I can finally tell you that you will have access to my own book. I gained confidence. With Dr. Bak as a mentor, I entered the Flow State.

Some access it naturally, others need structure. Once a force of nature is released, it is difficult to define its form. It can be at two extremes: peaceful as a breeze and mighty as a tornado.

To understand these mechanisms, we have to breakdown them, step by step. I thank Brenda for doing this wonderful work of mediating between Dr. Bak and myself. Indeed, I am sometimes incisive in my mission, because the goal is to find the secret of the secret: the trigger.

"Never settle for little, see the big picture.
Look for the latent potential."
Jonas Diop

We have established in this book that conditioning and the illusion of success can lead to internal crisis. Faced with our education and social pressure, three choices are available to us:

The first is to confirm ourselves there, to perhaps see our inner being die out with the force of monotony, never to discover who we are.

The second is to rebel, to make a 180 degree turn and reject, or even to be hostile to what we've learned.

The third choice is personal evolution, it is achieved when one shows a certain emotional maturity: to sort out what is useful to us, to become an eagle flying over its past with his eyes focused on the future.

In order to become an Alpha, in order to become a leader, it is first of all introspection, to take off this armor that has been grafted onto us, to learn to unlearn in order to finally know.

To trust, to have confidence, go against the small voice, the voice of doubt.

"Listen to your instinct
and not your conscience."
Jonas Diop

For us, the trigger occurred following friction, tension. At the time of this writing, there is an exceptional situation that leads to forced structural changes. People are waking up, people are in an identity crisis. The machine has slowed down, the matrix has bugged.

The truth is simple, we really need the help of an Alpha, not just to buildup confidence and charisma, but to guide us to escape fear.

We cannot force a person to follow a process or to evolve. However, we can provide him or her with the tools to do so, and above all, inspire them to take the first step.

This is what **ALPHA LADDERS** is about: to open the doors of hope for you to reach the better version of you. The volume one was about retracing our Alpha, Dr. Bak and what he has been through. The second tome will be about how can it serve you in your own journey.

> "Know yourself and know your enemy.
> In a hundred battles you cannot be defeated."
> Sun Tzu

Your own enemy is a mixture of fear, doubt, and conformity. Your own enemy is the one you look at in the mirror.

This book is an invitation to transform that reflection looking back at you into an ally. See beyond your appearance, beyond convenience. Know that your best imitation can never come close to your best version of yourself.

Walk your personal legend to rise.

This is **ALPHA LADDERS**, Captain of your destiny.

> DESTINY is not something we received,
> But something we write and rewrite
> Dr. BAK NGUYEN

CONCLUSION

by Dr BAK NGUYEN

Already, this is the end of this journey, the **ALPHA LADDERS'** journey. Joining forces with Jonas to guide you, from my awakening into my legend has been a pleasure.

To be honest, I had a very different book in mind as I made the cover and planned out the layout of this book. Well, loyal to my own philosophy, I emptied myself and proved once more the power of being flexible.

To all of you who follow me in my quests and legend, I must say that **ALPHA LADDERS** is one of my best work on personal growth and self-improvement. This is an understatement since revisiting my awakening and each of the steps leading to the building of my **TORNADO** allowed me to look back and to appreciate the journey so far.

Every time that I look back, I can't stand for long the view before I got vertigo. The first time happened after I received the award of **ACHIEVER OF THE YEARS** from LinkedIn Awards and TownHall. That took me a whole weekend to refocus forward and to regain my balance and momentum.

This time, it took 7 days. 7 days in which I allowed myself to look back and to share with you my past as a possibility of your future. What I did was not affected by vertigo since this time, it wasn't completely about my past, the part with *your future* kept me balanced.

If you yet needed another proof of the ladders of success, here's another one proving the power of compassion and generosity. That being said, I shared with you what I know, what I felt, and what I experienced being an Alpha.

"Being an Alpha isn't about what I want. It is not about being what I am either. It comes down to what I can do."
Dr. Bak Nguyen

And this is what is ahead for me. What more can I do? Sharing with you, I successfully inspired you to find your own quest, your story, your voice. I opened the door.

As mentioned many times during this journey, I have established myself as a leader and a champion driving hope and change. My mission is to change the world for the better. Haven't I told you that I am also very, very lazy? So how can I reconcile both of these together? Looking at you, of course.

If I want to keep changing the world on auto-pilot while keeping my engagement and authenticity, I must empower those amongst you with the same desire to rise and to walk your own legend. This is why I have to now grow into a great leader, not just a champion.

And what is a great leader? One empowering not followers but other leaders. I tried that organically, sharing with you my steps, but I have to realize that 3 years down the road, I may have inspired some of you to find your own voice, but I mostly have entertained you more than to empower you.

And now, we are back at the genesis of this journey, the **ALPHA LADDERS**. This is the heated conversation Jonas started a week ago in my office with Brenda as a mediator.

Retracing my own steps, I am ready to give you more. I will give you structures and templates to help you navigate through your own rise. I am doing that, despite my own taste. I hate structure. But one must face his results and see the truth.

This is not what I want. This is not who I am. But this is what I can do, for you. So be it. Let's do it."
Dr. Bak Nguyen

As Jonas shouldered me during **ALPHA LADDERS** looking for personal growth, mindsets, and recipes, I will have Brenda to join me on the next phase of this journey: the evolution from a legend into a community, **THE ALPHAS**.

In the next tome of this journey, I will submit myself to structuring a safe environment for you to find your voice, to exercise yourself safely and at your own pace to vibrate your frequency and, in time, to try the vibe of the frequencies of the Universe.

"I will show you. I won't force you.
But I won't wait for you."
Dr. Bak Nguyen & William Bak

Well, I can still live by those words, if I successfully build the blueprints and infrastructures that will outlast my presence. I am willing to give it a try, to structure, and to organize looking back, way back. I gave myself the same timeline I gave to any of my books: 14 days.

If my conversation with Jonas was all about me and my rise for your benefit, well, the journey with Brenda promises to be about neither you nor me, but about all of you, for the future emerging leaders of society. Very soon, I will welcome you into **ALPHAS LADDERS volume 2**.

Until then, let's take a time to celebrate our findings together, you, Jonas, and me. Do you realize that you hold in your hand a map to your own rise and legend? From listening to your frequency to emptying yourself to discover the powers of the Universe? We even mapped out for you the universal laws that you will be leveraging to ease your journey.

And you know what? It does not require anything special that you do not have. It requires only of you the desire to look for more about yourself and to take the time to give it a try, to give yourself a chance.

To each our own pace. To each our own personal journey. Besides that, the walk is often very similar and shares many common threads.

I must say that I envy you. I envy the excitement of discovering your true self for the first time. I envy the thrill of vibrating your first emotion to its fullest. I envy the intoxication of flying and rising. Sure I have those daily now, but the **FIRST TIME** is always special. Enjoy what is ahead and take the time to live fully those **FIRST TIME**. Then, you can relive them again and again at will.

"Power, to last through time and space has at its core compassion, the passion for others."
Dr. Bak Nguyen

This is **ALPHA LADDERS**, Captain of your destiny.

DESTINY is not something we received,
But something we write and rewrite
Dr. BAK NGUYEN

ABOUT THE AUTHORS

From Canada, **Dr BAK NGUYEN**, Nominee Ernst and Young Entrepreneur of the year, Grand Homage Lys DIVERSITY, and LinkedIn & TownHall Achiever of the year. Dr Bak is a cosmetic dentist, CEO and founder of Mdex & Co. His company is revolutionizing the dental field. Speaker and motivator, he wrote 72 books over 36 months accumulating many world records (to be officialized).

- **ENTREPRENEURSHIP**
- **LEADERSHIP**
- **QUEST OF IDENTITY**
- **DENTISTRY AND MEDICINE**
- **PARENTING**
- **CHILDREN BOOKS**
- **PHILOSOPHY**

In 2003, he founded Mdex, a dental company upon which in 2018, he launched the most ambitious private endeavour to reform the dental industry, Canada wide. Philosopher, he has close to his heart the quest of happiness of the people surrounding him, patients and colleagues alike. In 2020, he launched an International collaborative initiative named **THE ALPHAS** to share knowledge and for Entrepreneurs and Doctors to thrive through the Greatest Pandemic and Economic depression of our time.

In 2016, he co-found with Tranie Vo, Emotive World Incorporated, a tech research company to use technology to empower happiness and sharing. U.A.X. the ultimate audio experience is the landmark project on which the team is advancing, utilizing the technics of the movie industry and the advancement in ARTIFICIAL INTELLIGENCE to save the book industry and to upgrade the continuing education space.

These projects have allowed Dr Nguyen to attract interests from the international and diplomatic community and he is now the center of a global discussion in the wellbeing and the future of the health profession. It is in that matter that he shares his thoughts and encourages the health community to share their own stories.

"It's not worth it go through it alone! Together, we stand, alone, we fall."

Motivational speaker and serial entrepreneur, philosopher and author, from his own words, Dr Nguyen describes himself as a dentist by circumstances, an entrepreneur by nature and a communicator by passion.

He also holds recognitions from the Canadian Parliament and the Canadian Senate.

www.DrBakNguyen.com

From France, **JONAS DIOP**, Author-speaker, business strategist and leadership expert. Jonas Diop has already impacted the lives of entrepreneurs, high-level athletes as well as individuals thanks to his ability to awaken the best that lies dormant in everyone.

His mantra is always one step closer.

The so-called Empire Builder is known for his great energy and outspokenness, he is committed to ensuring that everyone can reach their full potential. Invested for over 15 years in personal growth, he has synthesized the essence of the best in their field in order to bring them to you.

Certified professional coach, NLP technician (Neuro-Linguistic Programming) He is also a member of the Club des entrepreneurs francophones du Canada.

Since 2017, he launched the podcast #DUC: Deviens Un Conquérant. From his atypical history, he knows the secret in order to achieve success.

www.JonasDiop.com

UAX

ULTIMATE AUDIO EXPERIENCE

A new way to learn and enjoy Audiobooks. Made to be entertaining while keeping the self-educational value of a book, UAX will appeal to both auditive and visual people. UAX is the blockbuster of the Audiobooks.

UAX will cover most of Dr Bak's books, and is now negotiating to bring more authors and more titles to the UAX concept. Now streaming on Spotify, Apple Music and available for download on all major music platforms. Give it a try today!

C O M B O
PAPERBACK/AUDIOBOOK
ACTIVATION

Please register your book to receive the link to your audiobook version. Register at:
https://baknguyen.com/ladders-registry

FROM THE SAME AUTHOR
Dr Bak Nguyen

www.**DrBakNguyen**.com

MAJOR LEAGUES' ACCESS

FACTEUR HUMAIN -032
LE LEADERSHIP DU SUCCÈS
par Dr. BAK NGUYEN & CHRISTIAN TRUDEAU

002 - **La Symphonie des Sens**
ENTREPREUNARIAT
par Dr. BAK NGUYEN

ehappyPedia -037
THE RISE OF THE UNICORN
BY Dr. BAK NGUYEN & Dr. JEAN DE SERRES

006 - **Industries Disruptors**
BY Dr .BAK NGUYEN

007 - **Changing the World
from a dental chair**
BY Dr. BAK NGUYEN

CHAMPION MINDSET -038
LEARNING TO WIN
BY Dr. BAK NGUYEN & CHRISTOPHE MULUMBA

008 - **The Power Behind the Alpha**
BY TRANIE VO & Dr. BAK NGUYEN

BRANDING DrBAK -039
BALANCING STRATEGY AND EMOTIONS
BY Dr. BAK NGUYEN

035 - **SELFMADE**
GRATITUDE AND HUMILITY
BY Dr. BAK NGUYEN

072 - **THE U.A.X. STORY**
THE ULTIMATE AUDIO EXPERIENCE
BY Dr. BAK NGUYEN

BUSINESS

SYMPHONY OF SKILLS -001
BY Dr. BAK NGUYEN

CHILDREN'S BOOK
with William Bak

The Trilogy of Legends

DENTISTRY

QUEST OF IDENTITY

LIFESTYLE

MILLION DOLLAR
MINDSET

PARENTING

PERSONAL GROWTH

PHILOSOPHY

THE POWER OF YES

SOCIETY

TITLES AVAILABLE AT

www.DrBakNguyen.com

AMAZON - BARNES & NOBLE - APPLE BOOKS - KINDLE
SPOTIFY - APPLE MUSIC

DR.

Bak Nguyen